Cross Connections, Fellow Travellers and Strange Bedfellows

by

Warren Lindsay Whaling

Cross Connections, Fellow Travellers and Strange Bedfellows

All Rights Reserved

Copyright © 2020 Warren Lindsay Whaling

Reproduction in any manner, in whole or in part,
in English or any other language, or otherwise,
without the written permission of the copyright holder is
prohibited

For information address

First Printing

ISBN: 978-0-6488645-8-5

Dedication

Sandra Elizabeth Whaling

I dedicate this book to my wife Sandra who shared a lifetime of experiences, memories, and connections, we now share with you.

Acknowledgements

Lorraine Rogers, Editor book structure, support and advice.

Barbra Bursill, Nina Bathersby and Leslie Organ for refreshing my memory of times past.

John Innes. For providing wartime background, decorations and photographs for Ian Rossell Capel Innes

Michael Hoggets for his contribution on the Great North Road.

Michael Davies for the final formatting and publishing the work.

Photographs:-

- Roads and Maritime Services – Roseville Bridge archive photos
- Cumberland Lodge – Aerial photograph
- Barbers and Surgeons – Great Hall and Reception Room
- Statues by Henry Moore – family archives
- Statues by Drago Marin Cherina – from a book of collected works

Cross Connections, Fellow Travellers and Strange Bedfellows

Introduction

We all have a life story to tell, and now, in my late seventies with time on my hands to reflect on family, happy memories, missed opportunity and misgivings, I have, with the benefit of hindsight, been looking back at a very full life. Today in retirement, with many around me in similar circumstances, I have come to realise how closely life paths of many of those new friends and acquaintances have crossed mine. It may have been association with other family members, similar friends, a place lived in or places visited. A missed appointment or phone call may well have sent you along a different life pathway. For me it has been all those and more. Essentially, we are all programmed to walk in a certain direction with a common destiny.

For a long time, I have had thoughts of writing my life story, if only as a record for future generations of my family. Now at the time of writing, the 2020 Covid-19 virus pandemic is sweeping the world. I am isolating in my home and using this time as an incentive to chronicle my memories.

I can relate to "Bacons Law" that suggests any two people are separated by no more than six points of personal contact. The realisation of my own immediate and near contact with significant world personalities and leaders has prompted me to document my own experiences.

Mark Twain once said "When I was a boy of 14, my father was so ignorant, I could hardly stand to have the old man around but when I got to be 21, I was astonished at how much he had learnt in seven years."

My father had an extremely strict upbringing and Twain's quote was true of the relationship between my father and me. I did not appreciate his contribution to my own persona until he passed away at the early age of 61. Alf, as he was known, ran away to sea at the age of 14 where he crewed as a deck hand, on the sailing Barquentine "Louis Theriault," trading timber around Asia and the Pacific and surviving a shipwreck off New Zealand. At the time of his death he could speak several languages, and had made a substantial contribution to the community, presiding over many public institutions and authorities. He was one of the founding members of the Australia Institute of Building, a Member of the New South Wales Board of Building Appeals, the Board of Subdivision Appeals, the NSW Building Regulations Advisory Committee, the Sydney City Markets Authority, Sydney Water Board and President of the Cumberland area Boy Scouts Association. He served on the NSW Government advisory panel for the Snowy Mountains Scheme and was President of Prospect County Council, now Energy Australia. Alf also served as President of the NSW and Local Government Association, Councillor on the Baulkham Hills Shire Council from 1953 to 1969, including President from 1953 to 1963 and he was also a guest lecturer on Local Government Law and Practice at Sydney University.

Alf was given a State funeral attended by the wider community and politicians of all persuasions. Following his funeral service at Castle Hill, a guard of Honour consisting of fellow members of Council and the Local Government Association was provided at the Church and Crematorium, together with a parade led by Boy Scouts, Girl Guides, Emergency Services and a Pipe Band, passing through Castle Hill. The main road was lined with constituents. The funeral cortege was preceded by a police motor-cycle escort all the way from Castle Hill to Northern Suburbs Crematorium with police traffic officers stationed on every major intersection.

A section of the A.H. Whaling Memorial Rose Gardens-
Roxborough Park Baulkham Hills NSW

The Baulkham Hills Shire Council dedicated 8000 square metres of land at Roxborough Park for the establishment of a memorial park, known as "The Alfred Henry Whaling Memorial Reserve," which includes an athletic field, Swimming Centre and Rose Gardens, opened by the Hon. Milton Morris MLC, Minister for Transport in 1972. Alf passed away on the 28th February 1969, a day before his sixty first birthday. With the average life expectancy now around eighty years, I often wonder what more he might have achieved if he had not been taken so early.

On one of his many overseas excursions around Asia, Alf was presented with a fez by President Sukarno of Indonesia. I now have the fez in my possession.

I recently finished reading R. M. Williams' book, "I ONCE MET A MAN," and found many similarities with their life stories. Both were born in 1908 and both left home at the age of fourteen to make their mark on the world. One attracted by the sea, the other by the Outback. Both were recognised for their contribution to the country following their passing.

The Barquentine Louis Theriault – Skipper, Captain Skinner

My father was also a strict disciplinarian. School holidays for me, meant working on his construction sites and in the joinery shop, learning basic skills, starting with that of "Billy Boy" fetching lunch orders for the workers and cleaning up after them before finally taking on the tools. However, he did have a compassionate and flamboyant side, particularly to his long term and loyal employees, assisting with building their homes and other necessities. At his funeral, my mother was approached by a woman, who had been deserted by her husband and left with young children to raise. She claimed that my father had helped to support her financially through difficult times. In those days, charity was the only option for people in those circumstances. Other than a small child endowment, there were none of the benefits available today. I am aware of a family friend in a similar situation, where my father provided her with a house for several years at Baulkham Hills.

Alf had a liking for fast cars. In the mid-fifties he imported a 304 Rover in which on one occasion, I travelled to Thredbo with my mother at the wheel. It was about 2 am, travelling towards Canberra at a hundred miles per hour beside Lake George, when headlights appeared approaching from the opposite direction, passed us, then the red braking lights illuminated, the vehicle turned around and followed us. There was little doubt as to their intention. My mother put her foot to the floor and the following headlights soon faded back into the distance. She, like my father, also enjoyed fast cars as well as skiing. Years later she became the proud owner of a Lagonda, one of only two in the country.

My introduction to the world of politics began when I was around ten years old. My father had completed the unit development at Parramatta for the New South Wales Housing Commission. I attended with him the official opening, undertaken by the Minister for Housing, the Hon. Clive Evatt QC, who unveiled the commemorative plaque. Clive was the brother of Labor Party opposition leader in the time of the Menzies Government, the Hon. Dr. H V Evatt QC. In the photo I stood beside the Hon. Member on his left, and on his right, his elder daughter Elizabeth, later to become Chief Justice of the High Court. My father and Clive became close friends. I can remember visiting their property in the Blue Mountains on a couple of occasions.

With Hon. Dr. Clive Evatt OC, MLC

Cr. Alfred H Whaling 1908-1969

Warren Lindsay Whaling MS. MRS. MIS (Aust)

My father had many friends on both side of the political scene and his one attempt to make a career in politics was when he stood for Liberal pre-selection for the Hills electorate North west of Sydney. His main opponent was Sir Garfield Barwick who won selection with the casting vote of Prime Minister, Bob Menzies. With the subsequent election we gave assistance at the polling booths for Sir Garfield, who also went on to become Chief Justice of the High Court after the close of his parliamentary term. Years later I joined the Liberal Party supporting notable State members like John Maddison QC and Nick Greiner. My father was a close friend of John Maddison, who also died at the early age of sixty, while still serving as the NSW Attorney General under the Askin, Wills and Lewis Governments.

I know little about my father's activities from 1925 until the end of the war in the Pacific in 1945. Old photographs show that he spent a lot of time around the Pacific and could make himself understood in several languages. I do know that he was in New Guinea in a role with the Australian government, but not with the military. After the war and before leaving government service, he and a friend Stan Woods, registered a business - SJ Wood & Co. Pty. Ltd. The partnership in the building company could not list my father's name, as he was still a Government employee and although he was the prime mover of the business and CEO, he never sought to change the name.

At the age of seventeen, upon completion of my school Leaving Certificate in 1958 at Macquarie Boys High School Parramatta, and uncertain as to my future direction, my father sent me to Townsville for three months to work on one of his building projects. Whilst there, I arranged to have a familiarisation flight in an Auster single wing aircraft. Following this I joined the Townsville Aero club and commenced flight training on Tiger Moths under instructor Jan Kingma, locally known as the "Flying Dutchman." The flight that day was also scheduled for a search and rescue mission to locate stranded stock and missing boats, following a cyclone that had devastated the area days before. The Criterion Hotel on the Strand where I was lodging also lost its roof. Jan Kingma and I were destined to cross paths again years later in the Snowy Mountains when I attended Cooma Airport for an aerial mapping flight.

On my return from Townsville I joined the Royal Aero Club at Bankstown to continue my training, where I flew de Havilland C1 Chipmunk training aircraft and achieved my first solo flight.

The de Havillands

Some years later, my wife Sandra and I became acquainted with Herroed and Jess de Havilland. Herroed's brother was Sir Geoffrey de Havilland OBE, who established the de Havilland Aircraft Company in the UK in the 1920s and later with Rolls Royce, played an essential part in the Battle of Britain, gaining British air superiority over Germany. Herroed and Jess had retired to Australia. They had built a large home in the country, opposite my in-laws at Baulkham Hills, west of Sydney. We frequently gathered around their pool for the regular Sunday "Pimms" before lunch. Olivia de Havilland and Joan Fontaine were daughters of Sir Geoffrey and nieces of Herroed and Jess. Olivia de

Havilland, star of "Gone with The Wind," only recently died at the grand age of 104 years.

A friend of my father, Sir Hudson Fysh, formerly partner to Sir Charles Kingsford Smith, arranged for me to join Qantas with a view to an aviation career. As it turned out, with a flood of Korean War RAAF pilots still looking for a similar career opportunity, I was facing a five-year delay before commencing flying training. Around the same time the opportunity arose to enter into Articles with a Registered Land Surveyor at Parramatta NSW, which eventually led to the opening of many doors and a career path gaining extensive experience in the professions of Surveying, Mining, Civil Engineering, Project Management, and other involvements ranging from the insurance industry, Industrial relations to International Diplomacy and the Wine Industry.

Rankine & Hill

In 1960 I gained a position with Rankine and Hill Civil and Structural Design and Consulting as a trainee Engineering Surveyor. The firm was then in a partnership with San Francisco based Design Engineers De Leuw Cather & Co., internationally recognised expressway design consultants. The two firms joined forces to undertake the design of the Warringah Expressway, linking the Bradfield Highway at Milsons Point, Sydney, to the Harbour Bridge. This was to be the first expressway project of its type in Australia, reclaiming a considerable area of North Sydney and Cammeray residential areas, including half of the Cammeray Golf course and my namesake, "Whaling Road". Prior to completion, the only access to the Harbour Bridge was via the Pacific/ Bradfield highway through North Sydney and a single lane entry from Neutral Bay at Milsons Point.

My initial assignment was to co-ordinate core sample drilling and logging and locating the position of exiting underground sewerage, water, telephone and gas services which frequently were not in the locations shown on the old service installation drawings provided, resulting in the inevitable service outage when we drilled through them.

Rankine and Hill were also responsible for much of the Road and Bridge design for the expanding Canberra, including the engineering for Lake Burley Griffin and the rowing course, of which I had personal involvement in the survey and set out before the Lake was filled.

The Snowy Mountains

In order to gain registration qualifications as a Land and Mining Surveyor from the NSW Board of Surveyors I was required to undertake a minimum of six months' experience with a country survey practice. My employer, Rankine and Hill had an association with a Berridale Survey and civil engineering firm, G F Hamm and Associates, to which they arranged transfer of my articles, with six months' leave of absence. As it turned out, my six months lasted for over three years.

*George Hamm was to later lead the Australian1968 Winter Antarctic mission to Mawson. He was a Chartered Surveyor, member of the Institute of Surveyors, (MIS) and Fellow of the Royal Geographical Society (FRGS) and Royal Astronomical Society (FRAS)."

Cross Connections, Fellow Travellers and Strange Bedfellows

I gained registration in 1966 and full membership to the Institution of Surveyors in 1970.

As a teenager, I had spent a great deal of time in the snowfields skiing, so I found myself in familiar territory. This was the time when the Snowy Mountains Scheme was at the peak of activity. Cooma became the headquarters for the Snowy Mountains Hydro-Electric Authority and thousands of workers descended on the regions from all corners of the globe to find work on the Scheme. Because of the isolation of the workplace and long working hours for the shift workers, usually working eleven days on and three days off, their focus for recreation was Cooma, which at the height of the scheme was host to some dozen or more night clubs that also benefited from the huge spend of the workers, attracting top shows from around Australia and overseas. The most notable or most popular was the "Pasha" Night Club which had the most popular act, a dancer whose only apparel was a carpet snake!

From my own experience, if you invited a lady to dine with you at a table for two, by midnight, you would be surrounded by a dozen mountain men trying to impress your lady. There were very few available women in town. The largest source was the female Snowy Corporation office staff who were accommodated in "Tinderry House", adjacent to the Snowy Corporation head office. This building, of course was always under heavy security, with the 10 o'clock curfew for visitors frequently broken, when many a "gentleman" was observed disappearing out of windows, at the sound of jackboots coming along the corridor.

These were wild and dangerous times in the mountains. 121 miners lost their lives in workplace accidents, mainly in the tunnels and underground excavations. A large proportion of the men were married and had left their wives and families back in their homeland with a view to earning enough money to send home for their financial support. Many wives eventually joined their husbands, settled in and contributed to our unique Australian story.

George Hamm's survey practice extensively covered an area from the Victorian border in the South, Hay, Balranald, Wagga Wagga in the West, to Canberra in the North, and over to the coast on the East: an area approximately ten percent of the whole of NSW.

This was matched by a large client base which included regional councils, Snowy Mountains Authority, Kosciusko Park Trust, Main Roads Department, Lands Department, CSIRO and private land holders.

From the office in Berridale, in the Snowy River Shire, survey parties were sent out to undertake a wide range of survey assignments. Up to this point in time the few isolated ski huts within the Kosciusko Park boundaries had no title, and therefore, no security of tenure, except for limited pastoral leases allowing summer grazing below the tree line. Those leases have since been extinguished.

This was a time when major corporations began taking an interest in the tourism and recreational value of the southern snowfields, so we were instructed to locate and map the position of all built structures and create a survey plan for a lease area incorporating the structure. This included the Kosciusko Chalet where I resided for several weeks with our survey party.

The Lease for the area of the Village of Thredbo was a major task with boundaries determined along the existing Road Profile and along the top of the Crackenback Range. Theodolite angular measurements were taken to the terminal points in order to calculate the side boundary measurement, without physically traversing the escarpment.

Adjustments were made for difference in altitude and observations to various mountain top trig stations to co-ordinate the survey within the NSW grid. To facilitate this, we also used pack horses to transport our equipment into the high country above the tree line, camping overnight under the stars and hobbling the horses to prevent them straying while we slept. There were no trees to tie a horse to and the rocks were ground smooth from the last Ice Age[1] 70,000 years ago. Amazing how far a hobbled horse can travel overnight!

As a backup for the accuracy of our measurements and calculations, the Australian Army asked us to test some new electronic distance measuring equipment it had recently acquired from overseas. The technology was based on the reflection of radio signals between two points and had not previously been used in this country. [2]

---

[1] The previous great ice age covering this area was estimated to last from 100,000 to 200,000 years ago

[2] The Tellurometer as it was known, used the reflected speed of sound to calculate distance, whereas current technology is based

The Monaro district was originally settled by a few squatters surviving on sheep, cattle grazing and agriculture. They had no tenure to the land they occupied until after 1820, when the Governor granted large parcels of land to them and other settlers. Free grants ended in 1825 following a direction from the Lord Chancellor in London that future allocation made, be with payment. The land was surveyed and subdivided by pioneering surveyors such as Parkinson and Busby, who cut through the rugged terrain and left their mark on many a tree to identify the boundaries of the land grants. Over one hundred years on, I was to find many of those marks by identifying the tree and cutting away a century or more of the growth over the original blaze, to find the Crown arrow cut into the original heartwood. Every time a marker was uncovered I felt an overwhelming sense of history and the hardship endured by those original surveyors and settlers living off the land, weeks away from any civilisation, with only a packhorse for transportation and on constant alert for unfriendly aboriginal hunters seeking to steal and kill their livestock. Sheep, cattle and horses were a much easier prey than wildlife. Those early survey plans were shown measured in chains and links and written description. When subdivided or altered, those Old System titles were brought under Torrens Title, requiring re-survey of

---

on the speed of light and is more recently the technology used for speed camera and satellite global positioning.

and converting the originally determined boundaries into feet and inches.[3]

Over the course of my stay in the mountains, I spent considerable time redefining many of those properties, and followed in the footsteps of those original pioneering Surveyors through bushland and rugged, "Man from Snowy River" country, that had changed little over time.

On May 17 1962, the sound of a currawong welcoming the dawn and despite the prospect of a sunny, warm autumn day, instead, I felt unusually despondent and lonely, for I had just woken up in a two man hike tent in the wilds of Michelago and it was my twenty first birthday.

For the previous few weeks our small survey crew had been breaking up the historic Ryrie Estate consisting of some 20,000 acres into smaller closer settlement allotments providing farming opportunities for ex-servicemen after the war. We camped on site rather than travel the long distance each day to and from the property. It would be another two weeks before I was able to celebrate my milestone at a Cooma nightclub with friends and colleagues.

NASA Connection

Of course, it was not all work. There was time for a range of recreational activities including trout fishing at Eucumbene, skiing at Perisher, Smiggins Hole or Thredbo, or just a quiet drink at the bar at the Berridale

---

[3] The metric system of measurement was not adopted in Australia until 1966.

Hotel, where one evening in April 1962, NASA launched into space a manned Mercury Rocket, with Alan Shepard on board. We were honoured to share this moment with three of the country's top physicists, Professor Harry Messel, and two of his colleagues. At their feet was the day's catch, a sugar bag full of trout. The three were huddled around the bar telephone with a direct line to Cape Canaveral Florida, awaiting the launch count down. Back in those days Australia led the world in radio astronomy and the development of radio-controlled air and space craft, so some of the Australian technology was playing a part in that event. My uncle Rex Burns was at the time the NASA liaison officer at the Parkes tracking station.

I had a special interest in their visit, as one of our commissions from the CSIRO was to set-out the Mills Cross radio telescope at Bungendore NSW, which was designed to search deep space looking for signs of extra-terrestrial signals, indicating other intelligent life. Because of the vast distance being searched, our ground measurement had to have extremely high order of accuracy, requiring pre and post standardisation of our equipment in the basement of the Sydney Lands Department, where the standard measure and constant temperature existed.

Rally Driver

Shortly after arriving in the Snowy and partly because of my youthful exuberance and adventurous nature, I became a member of the Snowy Mountains Sporting Car Club which among other things, managed the Snowy Mountains section of the Southern Cross

Rally, in the days when Ken Tubman was a notable rally driver.

I also held a Confederation of Motor Sport (CAMS) licence and drove in several rallies around southern NSW, one of which I won with my co-driver Harry Slater, the Snowy River Shire Engineer. Following the rally win, we retired to his home and after a few whiskeys, I fell asleep in front of a roaring fire, waking in the morning to the sound of a boiling kettle whistling away on the fuel stove. Entering the kitchen and exchanging pleasantries with my hosts, I took the kettle from the stove and placed it on my hand causing great consternation. A little useless trick that I had learned in my scouting days. The underside of a boiling pot is quite cold because the convection removes the heat as quickly as it is applied. One must remember to remove one's hand before the convection ceases! I also found time to play basketball for Cooma in the Group19 competition, which had us travelling to Canberra, Tumut, Wagga Wagga and other regional towns to compete.

Life Changing Connection

My first episode in the Snowy eventually came to an end when I fell victim to a common illness, mumps. I was forced to return to my parents' home in Castle Hill. There, early one Saturday morning, came a knock at the front door. I was the only one at home at the time and in my pyjamas, rose from my sickbed and opened the door. That very act was to be responsible for closing my page on the Snowy, although as destiny would have it, I was to return a few years later. For, at the door was one of my father's constituents seeking advice regarding the subdividing of his property. (My father being the Baulkham Hills Shire President had many similar requests). Standing alongside the visitor was his daughter, Sandra. From that first contact things moved very quickly. We were engaged six weeks later and married within a year. I returned briefly to Berridale to finalise my affairs and say my goodbyes. This closed my bachelor lifestyle of skiing, flying, motor sports, basketball etc. From this point on, my story would become a quite different one. Our story!

Only recently, when rambling through our collection of old memorabilia, I came across fifty old letters of mine I had sent to Sandra, my then fiancée, from Berridale during my final weeks before returning to Sydney. They became an essential source of material in awakening some of my memories. Reading them now, I cannot believe that I wrote them--must have had a ghost writer! I had been totally unaware that she had kept them all those years.

Despite the conditions, the Snowy Scheme was eventually completed within time and budget. A few years later, I returned with my wife Sandra, to the mountains to be involved in the construction of the last tunnel at Talbingo.

A Change of Direction

The extended stay in the mountains had delayed my studies and qualification, which I completed part time at NSW University whilst continuing to work in my profession. Now married with responsibility to provide for family, we built our first home on land I had purchased as a teenager at Baulkham Hills. Around that time, I followed up an advertisement for a position with John Holland Constructions as a surveyor on the Roseville Bridge, for which I applied and was successful.

The design of the bridge was extremely complex in survey and mathematical terms. Firstly, the abutment foundations and beams were angular and sloping and the profile a sweeping horizontal and vertical parabolic curve with superelevation and centreline variable offset. The original design was calculated on the country's first computer, occupying several levels of the NSW University building.

Upon setting out the first abutment, I soon came to realise that the Drawings supplied by the Department of Main Roads were inconsistent with the field measurements, bringing work to a sudden stop. The computer was wrong!

When John Holland Constructions signed the contract, they had assumed responsibility for the design, leaving the Department of Main Roads without any liability for the costs involved in recalculating or losses for the recalculation and construction delays. An ex-gratia payment was made on completion of the project.

Opening ceremony of the Roseville Bridge, 1966

Construction of the Roseville Bridge

I was charged with the job of re-calculating the dimensions, a massive undertaking of around three months. Without the use of computers as we now understand, I had at my disposal, a manual calculator and mathematical tables. Sufficient confirmation of the design had been completed to enable some construction work to recommence within a couple of weeks. On 2nd April 1966, the Roseville Bridge was opened after two years' work and the project management dispersed to other John Holland Projects around the country, some to Port Latter in Tasmania to construct the Iron Ore Terminal and some to Queensland.

Shortly before the completion of the bridge our son Anthony (Tony) Hugh Whaling came into our lives and we had just completed construction of our first home in Baulkham Hills, north west Sydney.

I remained in Sydney, with John Holland, to control the course of a sewage tunnel for the Water Board. This tunnel connected the southern metropolitan sewage treatment plant at Kurnell, dispersing some half a kilometre out to sea. This was another dangerous construction with the ocean threatening to break into the tunnel at any time. In fact, the last few metres had to be drilled by divers as the water rose gradually through fissures in the rock. Surveying under water did create a challenge.

Return to the Snowy Mountains

With the completion of the tunnel, I was reassigned to The John Holland head office, where I worked on the tendering for several projects, including the Talbingo diversion tunnel which we were successful in winning. I was assigned to the project as Engineer Surveyor under Project Manager, Rod King. My role was to establish tunnel entrances, control the alignment of the main and overflow tunnels, manage drilling pattern for explosives, manage 'Overbreak' and control aggregate stockpiles for the later concrete lining.

The Snowy Authority provided co-ordinates from the National Mapping grid and aerial photography ground stations, for the location of the tunnel entrance. There were no physical pegs in the ground as starting points, which I had to define using triangulation from mountain top trigonometric stations, such as Mount Kosciusko. Tunnel portals were located at the bottom of deep valleys.

Tunnelling proceeded from each portal. One at each end and one from 250 to 300 metres above high on the mountain side, were destined to become the future dam overflow. All were to meet deep down under the middle of the mountain at a bend in the tunnel. After six months of excavating and much to my relief, all tunnels met with a miss-close in the range of 10mm horizontal and 15mm vertical for the main and overflow tunnels. Heart attack territory when waiting for that final breakthrough- the sound of the drillers on the other side, which appears to be metres off alignment! Six months' work and the expenditure of millions of dollars had rested on my shoulders. Fortunately for me and my reputation, calculations, checking and rechecking had a positive outcome.

For the thirteen months of the project I had moved into a double-glazed weatherboard home relocated from Kiandra by the Snowy Authority. With me were my wife Sandra and our eighteen-month-old son Anthony (Tony). Talbingo was a town especially built for the Tunnel and construction of the Talbingo and Blowering dams. Town life was a little like the Wild West without the gunfights and the swinging bar doors.

  Large bonuses were earned by the miners who broke many world records for hard rock tunnelling. Cooma was several hours' drive away on the other side of the mountains and Tumut an hour's drive away. Therefore, recreation time was largely spent in the sole bar and café, often overcrowded. Sydney brothel owners saw a business opportunity and sent fully equipped Kombi vans to take advantage of the more amorous of the workforce. One evening after dining at the café, my wife observed a single light in the centre of the car park where a line of men had assembled. Sandra questioned as to why they were there, when a Kombi drove up, a man stepped out, quickly to be replaced by another. There were no further questions. On other occasions she would take Tony in stroller, to the shopping centre for groceries. On more than one occasion, workers took Tony into the café and plied him with ice cream and lollies. Many of these men from overseas missed family they had left behind whilst they earned the family fortune.

  The shopping centre remains today, while the original Snowy housing has largely been sold off and removed to become farm sheds, then replaced by modern homes. On the completion of the Scheme there was talk of the Authority and highly skilled engineers moving on to investigate the Bradfield scheme for diverting Northern rivers, inland. Fifty years on we are still waiting. Only once have I re-visited the mountains since.

With the completion of the Talbingo project, the CEO of John Holland, Geoff Cook, approached me to move to Melbourne. The company had just been approached by the Victorian Government to take over construction of the Westgate Bridge from the contract builders, World Services. A series of construction issues had arisen during the construction of the box girders which were buckling, due to excessive strain and for which World Services could not provide a solution.

Ted Moore

At the same time, I was approached by a former colleague, Edward (Ted) Moore, who was project manager for my first Holland assignment, the Roseville Bridge. Six months earlier, Ted had left Holland to start his own civil engineering company. He approached me to join him as a partner in his new enterprise, an offer which I accepted, leaving Holland and returning to our home in Baulkham Hills, Sydney. Shortly after Sally, our daughter, was born.

Fortunately for me, had I gone to Melbourne, I would have been on the Westgate Bridge, when on October 15, 1970, a span collapsed taking 35 lives, including project manager Ian Miller, a close associate of Ted's and mine. This sad event was a constant reminder of the inherent dangers with construction projects of this nature.

On a lighter note, I had sent flowers to Ian Miller's wife as a mark of respect for his death. At the time we were living in Wahroonga and my neighbours were also, Mr and Mrs Ian Miller. When I arrived home one evening, my wife Sandra was at the bottom of the stairs waving the invoice for the flowers. I had some explaining to do.

Ted and I remained in business together for the next twelve years until we were taken over by White Industries, which had won three major bridge contracts at Pheasants Nest on the southern freeway, south of Sydney.

E. M. Moore Pty Ltd. developed into a small team of a highly skilled workforce, capable of completing the most exacting engineering tasks. One of our most unusual projects was the design and construction of Concrete ammunition lighters for the Navy. Their purpose was to convey explosives and munitions from the Newington munitions storage facility on the Parramatta River, to supply naval ships in Sydney Harbour. Newington site later became part of the Olympic site. Their design required that they must be able to withstand a lightning strike and eliminated the possibility of an explosion.

We were successful with our second attempt. For the first, we were the only contractor to tender so the Navy recalled tenders, hoping to attract interest from other companies. The second tender had the same result and so the Navy contracted us to build the lighters. This was a million-dollar contract, a large sum for a small company in the early 1970s. We were required to supply five 300 tonne and four 500 tonne capacity vessels, which at capacity were to have a freeboard of no more the half a metre, to ensure that if there was an explosion in transit, the water would reduce any impact to any surrounding amenity. To reduce the possibility of a lightning induced electrical current, a stainless -steel plate was incorporated into the exterior of the concrete hull and connected to all metal components on the vessel for the earthing into the water.

For the construction we took over the disused Vanderfield & Reid timber yard fronting Blackwattle Bay, Balmain, where we constructed a slipway. Our first hurdle was to use our own workforce without raising the ire of the notorious Painters and Dockers Union who claimed all waterside work. It was only a matter of time before they realised what was happening and stormed onto the site, so we temporarily ceased operation. We were aware that the Union leaders would be attending a National Waterside Workers Federation Conference in Melbourne the following week, leaving only a receptionist at the Sydney offices. Knowing this, we sent our workers down to the Union office to be signed up to the Union while the executive was away. Understandably, they were a little upset at being outsmarted but could do little as their staff had signed them into the union. This was a time of the waterside wars in Melbourne resulting in the loss of life for several protagonists. We reached an amicable compromise by taking on one of the regular members, who of course would use his position to enforce any union practices on our men. Our solution was to give him the dirtiest job in the tidal zone, constructing the slipway. He left of his own accord two weeks later and we had no further trouble.

For the first 300 tonne vessel completed and ready to launch we arranged for a Standard tug to take control of the Lighter after launch.

500 tonne Lighter up for sale 2017

We all stood along the office balcony behind and above the slipway. The tug placed a large rope from the bow of the Lighter to the stern of the tug, slipway chocks were removed, and the vessel began slowly moving towards the water. Everything appeared to be going well but by the time the Lighter hit the water it had gathered some speed. Fully afloat, it sped past the tug, pulling it around 180 degrees and nearly pulling the tug underwater. Such was the inertia generated by 300 tonnes of speeding concrete! Lesson learnt; all remaining Lighters could float out into the bay without the tug attached until such time as it was appropriate to secure a line.

The Prime Minister

We were successful in being awarded many contracts with the Department of Housing and Construction, including marine works around Sydney

Harbour. One such project was a small jetty rebuild for Kirribilli House. Early one morning, after negotiating the usual security check, I proceeded down to the waterfront to inspect progress only to come across the Hon. John Gorton.[4] The Prime Minister and his wife were in residence, as signified by the flag flying at the entrance. He was out for an early morning stroll around the Gardens, still in his pyjamas and dressing gown. He beckoned me over and after a short chat we went our separate ways. Years later, Sandra and I were guests at an official Sydney Chamber of Consul Generals' function at Admiralty house next door.

Don Bursill & New Technology

Another project for the Department of Construction was the wineglass shaped water pressure tower at Tempe, intended to supply fire services at Kingsford Smith airport.

Built on a site high above the airport and approximately the height of a 15-storey building, the method of placement of the concrete would normally be by crane and bucket. However, we decided to use a new technology, the concrete pump.

A teenage skiing friend of mine, Don Bursill, designed the first piston drive concrete pump, delivering a continuous flow of concrete. At that time no one knew if you could deliver wet concrete fifteen storeys up. In the Snowy and Kurnell tunnels I had experience with air pressure pumps using compressed

---

[4] Hon. John Gorton served with distinction in the RAAF during WWII, and as Prime Minister 1968-1971.

air to push concrete hundreds of metres along a flat terrain.

We decided to trust Don's ingenuity and invested in his first pump that he had named T25, capable of delivering 25 cubic metres per hour. The use of concrete pumps is now common-place in the construction industry world-wide. Don's story does not end there, for he had many other ground-breaking achievements to his name which have changed the way we do things today. While writing this story, Don passed away. Like my wife Sandra, he had been languishing in a nursing home suffering from Parkinson's disease. Some individuals achieve notoriety by virtue of birth, wealth, creative or physical ability, while others quietly go about their lives constantly looking for a new challenge and not standing out from the crowd or seeking acknowledgement. Don fits into this category and his story should be told.

In the 1950s he attended Scots College in the eastern suburbs of Sydney, where the family lived. As an athlete he excelled, resulting in GPS and NSW State field track records still standing today, albeit similar distances are now measured in metres rather than yards. I can remember one of the stories from Scots, when he took a shortcut across the athletes' field one dark night on his way home and heard a number of thudding sounds around him, only to find out the next morning that someone practising archery had sent a number of arrows out into the darkness!

Don's interest in concrete technology did not come about by accident, as his family was responsible for introducing the Freyssinet anchor stressing systems to Australia. This revolutionary technology changed the construction industry around the world and is used in all large bridge and high-rise building construction.

Back in the period before electronic computers were available in Australia, he and a friend travelled to Japan and obtained some basic early model computers which they brought back to the country. Don eventually gained a reputation for computers and program development, his reputation spreading overseas and gaining the interest of a Casino owner in Istanbul. The Casino was losing money and the owner who believed that money was being siphoned off, contacted Don with a view to creating a program to manage the finances. Don and a mutual friend, Dr. Victor Zielinski went off to Turkey to computerise the casino operations. I lost contact with Don for a few years and when we reconnected, he had become the owner of the Istanbul Casino and had gone on to establish a further two casinos in Cyprus. Victor, with his wife Sue returned to Australia and established a get-a-way resort close to us in Lovedale, whilst continuing with his medical practice in Sydney. Readers may remember that with the introduction of the internet in the early 1990s, a roulette wheel appeared on a banner across the top of the screen. The wheel was from one of Don's Casinos on Cyprus. This would have made Don a pioneer of internet advertising.

Don eventually sold all his Casino operations and established a programming business, servicing casinos world- wide with more than 100 employees, then after remarrying, he retired to Guernsey in the Channel Islands. Sandra and I met up with Don in

London for dinner at the Regent Hotel one evening. A few years later, he and his new wife, "Woodie", flew in his helicopter to our winery in the Hunter Valley NSW, to re-connect and pick up some wine. He also had a substantial investment in a winery in Mudgee NSW and a helicopter charter business at Mascot Airport.

My original contact with Don was in my late teens, when I went on a skiing trip to Thredbo with my mother. We stayed at the or original Thredbo hotel and Don was nearby at Leo's Lodge. Other than a couple of ski clubs and a single chairlift, there was not a lot more at Thredbo. That trip created new friends who have remained throughout each of our lives, for I met Don in the bar one evening, together with Rick Rothpletz and Stephanie Plumber, an American citizen. None of us had met prior to that night. Within a couple of years, Don and I were groomsmen at Rick and Steph's wedding. A couple of years later, we attended Don and Barbara's nuptials. Steph's sister, Kathleen, is the mother of Matthew McConaughey of movie fame. Matthew, when nineteen years old, had stayed with Rick and Steph at their home in Elanora NSW for twelve months. Kathleen spent a few days with us in the Hunter and now lives in Texas with Matthew, his wife and three children. She still makes cameo appearances in his movies in roles similar to those of Alfred Hitchcock.

Liz and Ted Moore remained close friends until they both died in recent years. Many monuments stand as testament to our working relationship, to mention a few, the Roseville Bridge, five bridges over the Western freeway between St. Mary's and Penrith and the M1, Bulk wheat storages at Forbes and Trangie, and concrete water storage tanks and water structures around New South Wales and Queensland. I recently inspected one of our water storages that we built overlooking Lithgow and pleased to report is still a significant part of Lithgow's water supply infrastructure fifty years later.

Our civil business was eventually taken over by White Industries Pty. Ltd. Initially an earth moving and road construction company, they were successful in being awarded a contract for the construction of three major bridges on the southern freeway, the largest of which was the Pheasants Nest Bridge near Berrima. They did not have bridge-building expertise in-house, so they approached us to quickly fill the void, firstly as subcontractors, followed by an offer to take us over. On completion, Ted chose to try a new opportunity and I remained on for another two years as Civil Construction Manager for Marine and projects other than Special Projects, such as the Ulan Railway which came under the direction of the Mining Division. Ulan Mine was to become the largest open cut coal mine in the world, feeding coal out through the port of Newcastle, which in turn became the world's largest coal port, shipping over 100 million tonnes per annum. The growth of the company attracted the attention of Alan Bond, who made a raid on the company's shares listed on the Stock Exchange. With the value of the shares approaching $300, a substantial holding remained in the hands of Geoff White, company founder, together with directors, senior staff and committed associated entities. I had a few thousand shares, so we were asked to band together, to refuse the offer and hold off the raid on the company. My loyalty to the company was misplaced, as the Bond empire collapsed and so did the value of my shares.

James (Jim) Watson

During my time with White Industries, one of my Colleagues, Jim Watson O.A.M. JP, invited me to join the Committee of the St. Ives Horticultural and Agricultural Society, for the St. Ives Show. Jim was President for around twenty-five years up until his death in 1998. The show was a major three-day event held in March every year attracting up to 60,000 visitors. My role was Director of Entertainment which involved managing the "Showies" (sideshow attractions) and organising on field entertainment such as camel rides, pipe and other bands, Bush Fire Brigade, military displays and many more. Our Committee consisted of ten or so members. The organising for the Show required all of us to commit considerable time throughout the year to organise, particularly immediately the before and after setting and cleaning up.

Our show jumping events organised by Tony Robinson, attracted entrants from as far away as Western Australia and New Zealand, with the highest prize money in the country, apart from the Royal Sydney Show. Twice a year we partnered with the Windsor Polo Club to bring the sport to the area with notable players like Sinclair Hill and Michael Grace, together with players from New Zealand and Asia participating. Our major sponsor for the event was Bollinger, who supplied ample quantities of Champagne at a designated pavilion featuring black tie waiters carrying silver trays with flutes full of the desirable liquid. When a player came off his horse, the call was not "Where is the doctor?", but rather, "Quick, give him some Bollinger!" Polo is a particularly dangerous sport, so there was always a medical team on hand as well.

James Henry Watson O.A.M. JP died on April 30, 1998. The main arena at the St Ives showground is named in his honour. He was also on the executive of the RSL for many years.

My role lasted for seventeen years up to the time we permanently relocated to the Hunter in 1994. Fellow committee member Malcolm Scott, who organised the polo, together with John and Sally Warne, Sandra and I moved to the Hunter Valley where we all again came together to form the Hunter Valley Polo Association in conjunction with the Wirragulla and Scone Polo Clubs.

I left White Industries after completion of the Boondooma Dam, West of Brisbane in Queensland, following my acceptance of an offer to Join Girvan Bros NSW Pty. Ltd. as Director, Construction Manager.

Sandra

My wife Sandra was not standing still while I was gallivanting around the countryside. Having not worked for several years she took a job with Peterson's of Pymble where she remained until the property was sold for redevelopment. Peterson's was the last of Sydney's General stores where you could buy anything from ladies' high fashion, Gentlemen's outfitters, school uniforms and electrical goods to builders' hardware. One of the more unusual products they stocked, was gelignite and detonators, which were stored in an explosives box behind the car park. When one of our projects involved hard rock excavation, I would run down to Peterson's and fill up the boot with explosives before heading off to deliver them to the site, although we were required to show an explosives licence. Could you imagine doing the same today? My father also used the occasional stick of "Gelly," for the removal of the odd stump on their property. This was much easier than digging it out by hand and it had a side benefit of fertilising the ground with nitrogen, ready for a new planting. You would just make a deep hole with a bar, slip a stick of "Gelly" down, light the fuse and stand back.

Sandra then moved on to a fabric retailer in Chatswood before linking up with "Fabrica" owner Trish, who had outlets in Turramurra and Woollahra. Together, they went to Thailand to buy Thai Silks from Jim Thompson Silks. There is a great deal of history and mystery around the Legendary Jim Thompson. He was parachuted into neighbouring Burma shortly before the end of the World War 2 to stabilise American influence in the region. In private life he was a well-known architect before joining the US army and eventually becoming a member of the OSS, forerunner to the CIA. Returning after the war, he bought a half share in the Oriental Hotel, which later, was refurbished to become one of the most desired destinations in Asia. At the same time, he took an interest in the un-coordinated, Thai silk weavers, bringing them together to form a collective and introduced them to European colour fixed dyes. (They had previously used non-colour-fast vegetable dyes.)

He is remembered as the saviour and "king" of the Thai silk industry.

It is believed Jim Thompson remained an agent with the OSS until his death. This was a time when the communist insurgency was at its peak. He had gone to the Cameroon Highlands, in the Pahang district of Malaysia, supposedly for an Easter holiday. On the Sunday afternoon his hosts, while resting, heard him leave the house, assuming he was going for a walk, but he never returned. He was an experienced bushman and knew the area well. Heavy jungle surrounded the holiday cottage with only one access road. Intensive searches revealed nothing, creating the theory that he was spirited away because of his OSS connections.

Thompson Silks featured in the 'King and I', which brings me to the point of my story. Sandra and Trish met with Bill Booth, who had taken over the running of the Thai silk business after the disappearance of Thompson. He invited them to dinner at his "Campong" located on the upper level of a high-rise building in Bangkok, immediately above the New Zealand Embassy. Two Thai military guards stood outside the door with automatic weapons slung over their shoulders. They were a male and a female, holding hands, but otherwise at the ready. Inside they were introduced to Bill's wife in full Thai National Dress, then the children were introduced one by one, the youngest to the eldest, like the famous scene in the 'King and I'. Bill Booth had converted to Buddhism and married a Thai princess. Jim Thompson's home, which he built in the classic Thai style, influenced a return to Thai architecture and remains a National Treasure.

Sandra worked for fashion designer Carla Zampatti, in her Mosman shop, where she became acquainted with Marianne Hobbs, and on meeting her husband John Hobbs, we readily became friends, as I was already friendly with his brother Keith. John was close to retirement from CASA, the Australian Air Safety Authority, where he was chief check pilot. CASA and Qantas gave him a big send-off at the North Sydney Travelodge, attended by the Federal Aviation minister and senior pilots from all major airlines. John was also invited by Qantas to fly with their first 747B Jumbo Jet from Seattle, Washington to Sydney. John had served with the RAF during the war and he piloted the Vulcan bomber that delivered the first atom bomb from England to Maralinga in the remote western area of South Australia. John and Marianne retired to Maroochydore in Queensland.

Sandra also accompanied me on a Trade mission to Asia and Australian wine shows in Dublin and London.

The Next Ten Years

I joined Girvan in 1984. The company was a medium sized Builder with subsidiaries in equipment hire and shopping centre management. This was a time when building design for high rise structures were undergoing radical changes, with the introduction of light weight curtain wall cladding and together with solar panel technology, were relatively new to Australia. Girvan was at the forefront of adapting to these changes and we caught the attention of one of the larger Japanese construction companies, Obayashi Corporation, which was in the forefront of developing prototype building systems in their laboratories, situated just out of Tokyo. I was introduced to their Overseas Development Manager, Nobio Ito, who made several regular trips to Australia, with a view to marketing their systems.

Nobio Ito

Nobio and I became close friends, meeting for breakfast at the Wentworth Hotel on the occasions of his visits to Sydney. He was educated in Oxford before the war and he spoke the Queen's English. He was called up by his country to fight against the Allies and drafted into the Japanese air force and referred to himself as a retired Kamikaze pilot. The war ended before he got the call. His friendship gave me an insight into Japanese culture that hitherto I was unaware of, although my mother and father had visited there during the occupation. Japanese was one of the languages my father picked up in his days sailing the Pacific.

1984

In 1984, Nobio invited me to inspect the Obayashi Gumi experimental facilities in Japan and together with Sandra and daughter Sally we booked a trip. After arrival at Narita Airport we transferred to the Keio Plaza Hotel at Shinjuku, Japan's main rail terminal catering for eight million passenger transfers a day at that time. It was a remarkably busy place.

The following day, I was picked up by a stretch limousine arranged for me by the company. I had planned for Sandra and Sally to take a rail trip up to the ancient city of Nikko, whilst I was engaged with my hosts. The facility out in the countryside, was an hour's drive from the hotel. The drive through crowded suburbs and roads choked with traffic was somewhat enlightening. However, I was comfortable in the armchair seat at the rear of the limousine, complete with bar and telephone at my disposal. On arrival I was directed into a small room where it was requested that I sign the guest book located on a coffee table in the centre of the room. Sitting down on the leather lounge, I scanned the guest book open to a blank double page, which the attendant gestured me to sign. Initially my thoughts were to sign the left-hand page at the top allowing room for others to follow. I turned the page back to view the previous guests in order to follow likewise. Across the two pages was the signature of the Aga Khan1V. (Prince Shah Karim al- Hasseine). I turned the page back and did the same.

The experimental building was far advanced to anything I had seen in Australia. One was built with curtain walling, window double glass and reflective with shutters fitted outside that automatically followed the sun to control lighting and heat. Panels on the roof produced power and hot water that was stored in underground coils to heat the building during the cold winters. No power was supplied from the outside power grid, as everything was generated internally. There were around one hundred technologies being investigated within the facility. I was very much impressed.

Sally, our daughter, was asked if she would like to stay in Japan for a year on exchange while Sandra and I were to take a Japanese student for a similar period. Unfortunately, we could not convince her to accept- a decision which she has since indicated some regret. She also refused an offer to marry a young Japanese youth, on the side of Mount Fuji. We were impressed with the politeness of Japanese society and questioned why after years of allied occupation they had a great respect for General Douglas MacArthur. The answer was simple. MacArthur destroyed the power and tradition of the Samurai and the War Lords, ruled with a firm hand without oppression, won over the support of the Emperor, distributed land to the populace and created a new constitution for Japan, which they still respect.

We had the opportunity to tour much of the main Island before flying out to Taiwan. Our travels took us to Fuji, Hakone, Nagoya via the bullet train and out to Shima, Kyoto and finally out via Osaka. Kyoto was the ancient capital of Japan with beautiful shrines and gardens. Before the end of the war the Americans declared it a heritage city, leaving it intact and protected from allied bombing, unlike Hiroshima and Nagasaki after their nuclear destruction and the carpet bombing of Tokyo and most other regional cities.

Taiwan.

Ever since General Chiang Kia-Shek retreated in exile from mainland China for relative safety under the umbrella of American protection, there has been a state of war between the Nationalists and the mainland Communist regime. Landing at Taipei airport, the evidence of high security was everywhere with the constant threat of invasion from the mainland. We had visas to enter, although our passports were not stamped on entry or exits, as we were to complete our

Cross Connections, Fellow Travellers and Strange Bedfellows

trip with a visit to Mainland China via Hong Kong. This visit would not have been possible had the passports shown a Taiwanese endorsement.

The indigenous people of Taiwan have features and a culture of dress and living in tepees, like the American Indians and Polynesians. The mountainous region of Taiwan contains more than thirty peaks approximately twice the height of Mt Kosciusko. They form a border between the industrialised alluvial plains on the west and the narrow plains facing the Pacific Ocean on the east. We caught a CAC Airlines' DC3 from Taipei to the west coast town of Hualien. The three of us were the only English- speaking people on the bumpy, no- frills flight. Coming into land, the hostess made an announcement in Mandarin 'hoping that passengers had enjoyed their flight', then for our sake, repeated in English," I hope you have enjoyed your fright." From the air, the Airport on which we were about to land had little to show of its real purpose. The logistics of the airfield resembled more of an aircraft carrier than a quiet country airport. Beneath the ground, were fighter aircraft that could be raised to the surface in minutes and factories capable of aircraft manufacture, deep within the mountains behind the airport. Security at Taipei and Hualien was intense with pat-down searches both ends. Even the lens was taken out of my camera!

Our destination was the Taroko Gorge, Asia's Grand Canyon, set among towering marble cliffs and cascading waterfalls. The fifteen kilometre, hair-raising drive up the Gorge, went along a single lane road with few passing lanes. At one point, a bus came from the opposite direction. We alighted to walk behind the bus which drove within a metre of a sheer drop of several hundred metres to the river below. The drivers were obviously familiar with this procedure. The passengers were not! There were no safety rails. The Gorge ended at the base of an even higher mountain with thermal springs, waterfalls, exotic plants and lots of monkeys ready to carry off anything they could get hold of. We then were faced with the prospect of the trip back down.

We had the opportunity to visit the National Museum where many of China's historic treasures are stored in caves within the mountain behind, twenty percent of which are on display on rotation for three months at a time. Chiang Kai-shek brought the treasures with him on his escape to Taiwan. Some of the antiques date back many thousands of years, The Chinese Government, would love to have them back. Taiwan was Japanese territory prior to the second World War and under the administration of General MacArthur, until the conclusion of the Korean War. Any claims for sovereignty by China using force, would likely elicit a response from the West. China has long chosen a strategy to try to isolate Taiwan within the international community. Today, in 2020, Taiwan is again the focus of international tension, with China becoming more aggressive and belligerent to all its neighbours around the South China Sea.

Our short stay in Taiwan came to an end. However, I was to return years later, on two occasions, representing BHP and Newcastle as part of NSW Government Trade Missions into Asia. Sally also visited with another mission, which focused on New

Zealand and the Pacific, representing the local Hunter Valley Wine Industry.

China

Following an accord with the United States, China partially opened its doors to western visitors in 1978. Our entry into China in September 1984 was still viewed with suspicion by the Chinese authorities. Our passports were confiscated on entry, leaving us uncertain as to our immediate future. We did go on to be one of the first users of American Express in China and received our passports back on exit via Macau, obviously scrutinised for any evidence that we had landed in Taiwan.

Back to Business

In the days when I was with White Industries, I represented the company's membership on committees of the Federation of Civil Engineering Contractors Australia, however Girvan was a building concern and I was to represent them on the Industrial Relations Committee of the Master Builders Association of New South Wales. Some companies were members of both organisations. The Builders Labourers Federation was heavily committed to creating disruption in the industry with heavy handed, many criminal, intrusions onto workplaces, costing the industry and the community hundreds of millions of dollars. A small sub-committee of the MBA was charged with the role of applying for deregistration of the Union. I was a member of that sub-committee. Our endeavours finally proved successful and the Industry enjoyed relative peace for several years following. I had a good relationship with the executive of the New South Wales Trades and Labour Council. For the most part I respected their common sense and they respected my even handed dealing of issues that came to their attention, so much so that with the agreement of the MBA, I was nominated to arbitrate between employers and member unions on a number of disputes. The Arbitration Act required that an arbitrator's decision be final, and his/her determinations cannot be appealed except for a proven error in law. Many of the T&LC executives were later to take up senior positions in industry.

One landmark Girvan Development was the Toowong Shopping Centre, a short distance from metropolitan Brisbane. The company purchased properties adjacent to the Toowong railway station and submitted a development proposal to the Queensland Government to redevelop the site including the air space over the adjacent railway station. This provided for extending the shopping centre above and a total reconstruction of the station. This was back in the Joh Bjelke-Petersen days. The Government pushed the project through parliament in the early hours of one morning in 1984, paving the way for the development to proceed.

My role in overseeing the approval and planning process, ended with the appointment of a Project Manager to the project. Girvan had entered contracts for the lease of space on completion of the two-and-a-half-year construction period. The key tenant was to be David Jones, occupying two floors of the Centre. Their contract guaranteed a completion date, with penalties of half a million per week for late completion. Construction work progressed uneventfully for the first twelve months before the unions began to take an interest in the project. After eighteen months, the project was running three months behind program. The unions were running rampant with unsustainable demands and constant strikes. Subcontractors also joined the fray with claims for "Extra works" and within a few months the project had virtually ground to a halt, requiring substantial changes to management.

    I was sent back to Brisbane to co-ordinate all construction activities and another colleague to co-ordinate the tenancies and fit outs. My first job was to sit down with Union leaders and convince them that it was in their interest to come on side and get the men back to work, which I achieved within the next two weeks. As for the subcontractors, I had assured them that I would negotiate their claims immediately site production had recommenced. Many of those claims were ambit claims amounting to a total of $3.30 million. All claims were eventually settled for a little over $770,000. However, the project was still running three months behind program, with six months left to complete, and a potential damage claim by David Jones for seven million dollars, which meant that the project had to be accelerated. I contacted our electrical subcontractor Kevin R Sheather Electrical, a company with divisions in several states including Queensland and who were engaged on the project with limited ability to provide additional resources from their Queensland branch. I rang Kevin Sheather in Sydney, saying "I need twenty additional electricians, and I need them tomorrow". The Following day I had twenty new faces on site. A similar request was made of all services and finishing trades. A week out we still had three weeks' work left to complete. Our only option was to work around the clock with workers taking rest breaks sleeping on the newly laid carpet. With three levels of scaffolding remaining in the main atrium, I would walk through the centre stepping over prostrate bodies asleep on the floor.

Much to the relief of everyone, the intense effort paid dividends and the official opening was held on the day contracted three years earlier. I had been without sleep for the previous three days, so retreated to my hotel for some shuteye.

Schematic drawing of the proposed shopping centre and Railway Station.

A few weeks later I was approached by Australian Airlines and advised that I was the most flown person between Sydney and Brisbane over the previous six months, travelling back and forth at least twice a week. I still had contractual commitments in Sydney to attend to.

In recognition of our loyalty and with six other frequent flyers from other destinations, we were flown to South Australia for the day for a private luncheon in the Henschke Cellars. Sandra was not particularly impressed, not because she was not invited but, because all male invitees were each accompanied by a personal hostie for the day. We all enjoyed the lunch, the trip each way and the company.

Peppers Group

Mike and Suzi O'Connor opened Peppers Guest House, at Pokolbin in the Hunter Valley in 1984, followed by "The Convent" in 1991, a joint venture with James Fairfax and restaurateurs Robert and Sally Molines, from Roberts Restaurant. "The Convent," once the home of the Brigidine nuns in Coonamble, was transported about 600 kilometres to Pokolbin in three sections and was re-erected, complete with "Ghost" (thought to be Mother Superior) on the Halls Road site. Before completion, the security company's dogs would not enter the building!

These events influenced my future direction in several ways. Sandra and I were among the original guests at both the Guest House and The Convent, where we had booked all rooms for our daughter Sally's Hunter Valley wedding. Also later, with Girvan, I attended the first conference to be held at Peppers Guest House.

The Girvan Association, together with Mike and Suzi O'Connor, saw the seeds of the Peppers Group's third resort development come to fruition when they joined in a partnership to develop the old Terrigal Hotel site to become "Peppers on Sea". The development, completed in the late 1980s, was designed and constructed by the Girvan Group, as owner. The interior design and furniture fit-out was under the direction of Suzi O'Connor and the Peppers Group, as resort managers. The hotel, which was later sold to the Mantra Group to become known as the "Crowne Plaza Terrigal", is of classic design with wide sweeping staircases to foyer level, standing the test of time and several refurbishments. The hotel remains one of the country's most desired accommodation destinations.

With the conclusion of my Queensland activities, I took over the role of Construction Director for completion of the project. The old Terrigal Hotel which was demolished to make way for the new resort had a reputation as the venue for the annual NSW Labor Party convention. We did search for a few skeletons in the closets, but could not find any to speak of, except for a few rumours and innuendos.

The Peppers Group went on to develop and operate several upmarket accommodation hotels and resorts around Australia, New Zealand and Asia Pacific, but is now controlled by the International Mantra Group.

Industrial Relations

Girvan was a member of the Master builders Association and part of my role was to represent the company's interest within that organisation. Years earlier I had a similar role with the Australian Federation of Civil Engineering contractors, while I was working with White Industries. The main role of the Industry organisations was to act on behalf of members in collective negotiations with Union Award claims, disputes and Industrial Commission hearings. The construction industry has always been a hotbed of industrial unrest. With so many players in the market it has been relatively easy for construction unions to pick off employers one by one using one means or another, legal and illegal. I have seen many instances where Union enforcers have coerced, physically threatened and black- mailed smaller unrepresented sub-contractors who were intimidated into paying "Union Fines" for not following Union directives. Unfortunately, many of the larger construction companies allowed themselves to become complicit when told by unions not to engage uncompliant sub-contractors in the hope of industrial peace on their building sites.

A personal example of Union exploitation of the workplace was on a refurbishment of Roselands Shopping Centre when the Builder labourers pulled their members off the site claiming that asbestos had been found. The normal procedure would require the contaminated area to be isolated and for the hazardous material removed by trained and accredited personnel. As it turned out we had evidence that the site had been "salted" with asbestos. The men were called out for two weeks, with the Union demanding full payment of wages while on strike. I refused their demands and after a month on strike the workers approached me directly agreeing to return to work without payment. The contract was completed without further delay. That Union gave me a wide berth thereafter and chose to take on softer targets. I did have the support of the New South Wales Trades and Labour Council, who with the MBA nominated me to arbitrate on other industrial issues.

      The Builders Labourers' Federation was one of the worst rogue unions inflicting huge financial damage on the industry and wider community. I was a member of the New South Wales MBA industrial relations committee which, in association with the Victorian branch of the MBA, applied to the Industry regulator for deregistration of the union. This process took several years before the Union was finally deregistered in 1986 with the main players joining the Building Workers Industrial Union (BWIU) which at the time was a relatively law-abiding organisation. Following deregistration, the industry enjoyed a few years' relative peace and co-existence with the Union movement. The 1992 Giles Royal Commission into productivity in the building industry was to identify many practices by Companies and Unions detrimental to industry behaviour. As an interested party, a taxi would arrive at my address every Monday over the course of the hearings, delivering transcripts of the previous week's proceedings.

Ian Innes and More New Technology

Girvan grew into a major publicly-listed Corporation. I was to hold directorships with several subsidiary companies. One of those, "Corporate Direction," was responsible for Legal compliance, Training, Health and Safety, Industrial Relations, Contract scrutiny, intervention and resolving of commercial disputes, as well as looking for new opportunities.

One day, a gentleman made an appointment to meet me at my office in Chatswood. Ian Innes arrived with his son John and placed before me a proposal to invest in a new untested computer technology, based on the Legal and Insurance Industries. Ian had a lifetime of experience in the Insurance industry and with his son John Innes, they had developed new generation thinking computer programmes that could track fraud. They had exhausted their efforts to convince the major insurance companies to back their product in which they had already invested $3 million of their own money.

We had protracted discussions before I fully understood the possibilities and involved one of our main group Board directors. We placed a proposal before the Board to take a fifty percent stake in the company, Innes Owens Pty Ltd, by purchasing the shares held by New Zealand Investor, Doug Owens. The proposal was adopted and over the next couple of years Girvan invested around $8 million into the development of the program. New subsidiaries within Innes Owens Pty Ltd, included Innes Owens Insurance Pty Ltd and Innes Owens Workers Compensation Pty.

Ltd. I was appointed to all Boards to represent Girvan's interest.

Computer programming always requires more time and more funding than anticipated. However, we reached a point where we had developed a product ready to market to industry. The main attraction was a huge data base of medical and legal outcomes from Australia and the US, with the ability to track workplace injury, create a path for recovery and potentially detect fraudulent activity.

At the time there were twelve licensed Workers Compensation Insurers in New South Wales. We made an application to the New South Wales Workers Compensation Commission for the issuing of a licence. After a due diligence process by the Government, we were awarded the States' thirteenth licence. Within two years we had gone from number thirteen insurer, based on policies written and value of funds held in Trust on behalf of the Government, to third position.

There were other opportunities that arose for the business. I was also a member of the MBA Industrial Relations Committee. A proposal was presented before them to arrange a meeting with the NSW Trades and Labour Council, together with Innes Owens executive, where we placed before them an initiative for managing a process to assist injured workers to return to work as quickly as possible. Both organisations came on-board and that meeting created a collaboration that remains today and is adopted by many other States. The Australian Taxation Office also bought the programs to isolate fraud within their systems.

During that time, we started negotiating with Ross Perot, who later, in 1992, ran unsuccessfully as an independent US Presidential candidate. Ross was a high-powered Industrialist in the United States with interests in the Insurance Industry.

In 1985 Sandra and I purchased our property in the Hunter Valley, and in the following year we sold our home in Wahroonga and purchased a town house in Kurraba Road, Neutral Bay, where we lived for the next six years, travelling most weekends to the Hunter.

One morning in 1989, my neighbour Paul Reading, who knew me as Lindsay, my second Christian name, approached me asking if I had a brother named Warren. My response was, 'No, that is me.' He had in his hand documents relating to the sale of Girvan subsidiary, Trivan Plant Hire Pty Ltd., a company of which I was a Director, being sold to ANI/Coates Plant Hire Pty Ltd, a company within the Packer empire of which he was a Director. The sale was arranged by the main Girvan Group Board of which I was not a Director and I had no knowledge of the sale. The sale documents did contain my name giving guarantees providing for continuing plant hire by the Girvan construction companies. I had no prior knowledge of the sale and immediately resigned as an employee and Director, with the exception of Innes Owens, where I retained my Director positions for another six months until the Girvan Holdings were sold on to C. E Heath Casualty and General. It is now part of the IAG Insurance group, running their CGU Workers Compensation business based at Pyrmont, where we started thirty-five years ago. The deal with Ross Perot was signed and sealed shortly after.

The breakthrough technology was also licensed to Work-Cover Queensland and to this day runs all workers' compensation claims, common law claims and injury management for the State of Queensland.

The US rights were sold to a joint venture led by Perot Systems Corporation and these systems today drive leading self- insured corporations such as Boeing, American Airlines, Publix Supermarkets, The City of New York and many Insurance Companies writing workers' Compensation Policies.

Ian Rossell Capel Innes. Mm. Chev LdH.

Ian and Gwen Innes remained close friends of ours for many years with the occasional dinner at Lees Fortuna Court at Crow's Nest, where Ian had permanently reserved a table in one corner of the room and retired Federal member of parliament Graham Richardson (Richo), in another. Our relationship with Lees Fortuna was not only one of regular patronage going back to the seventies when they started in North Sydney, we also had our wine on the wine list for nearly 30 years. Both Ian and Gwen died in 2019; Ian at the age of 98 years. Ian was a WW2 veteran, awarded France's most distinguished Medal, The Legion of Honour in 2015, in recognition of his wartime service and awarded also, the Military Medal for his service behind enemy lines. He was a bombing aimer and back up pilot in the '78 Bomber squadron' when his plane was shot down over France. Their target that night had been the railheads at Laon near Mailly-Le-Camp, which had been a French army training camp. It was taken over by the German Army following Occupation, turning it into a tank training centre and home for the

21st Panza Division, an important target ahead of the advancing Allied forces.

Heading home, their Halifax bomber became the victim of Luftwaffe night fighters over Rubescourt near Farm de Pas (115 km north of Paris). Most of the rear-gunners' turret and wing tanks were blown away by the night fighters' Schrage Canons, causing fire and explosions on the plane. Ian and the navigator forced a jammed nose escape hatch, before exiting from the aircraft. All crew escaped the plane by parachute, most ending up in the hands of the Germans to see out the war in concentration camps. Ian parachuted into the backyard of a tavern, breaking his toe on landing having lost his boots in the slipstream. He hid there, undetected until the next morning. Surviving the ordeal, and using his limited French, he was hidden by the French underground movement for three months, constantly moving location to avoid capture by the Germans. His aim was to reach the Swiss border and find his way back to England. However, the Resistance linked him up with a small well- armed British SAS unit operating deep behind enemy lines. The unit was commanded by Captain Grant Hibbert (DSO). Together with another downed American flyer, they offered their services to the unit. Well supplied from the air, their role was to frustrate the German retreat, hitting hard and disappearing into the bush. One such attack inflicted 500 German casualties with only one SAS killed and two wounded. The deceased SAS officer in full uniform, was left for the Germans to find to divert any suspicion that locals Were responsible with the consequence of reprisals. Ian eventually made his way back to England shortly before the end of the war, when he was promoted to Pilot Officer and awarded the Military Medal. Since the end of the war he made many a pilgrimage back to France to see the many partisans who had befriended and protected him. It was a privilege to have known him and to have played a small part in his life story, and with him, giving my own contribution to the changing world of workers' compensation.

RAAF Badge

French Legion of Honour

The Halifax Bomber

Ian Rossell Capel Innes

Dragon Boats

As an employee of Girvan it was not all business. The physical and mental fitness of the whole family were considered an essential component of bonding corporate culture. Group personal development by way of technical training, conferences, annual medical check-ups, Gym memberships, sports trainers were all part of those activities designed to stimulate a competitive environment within the group and externally. A number of other corporations with a similar outlook came together at the invitation of the promoter Standard Chartered Bank, to bring Dragon Boat racing to Australia.

For this, specially built racing boats were brought in from Hong Kong and company crews began training for the first national event at Sydney Cove in 1985 where crews from Girvan, Lend Lease, State Bank, Ipoh Hardens, Lang & Wootton, Manly Surf Club and Standard Chartered among others competed for the title with the overall winner, the Manly Surf Club, going on to represent Australia in Hong Kong. The Girvan team came a close second "with the anchor dragging". Had we won; the greater part of management would have disappeared to Asia for a couple of weeks. We did win the final of the mixed team races. No gold or silver medals were handed around, but we did receive a banner for our effort. Each team consisted of twenty paddlers, a drummer to keep stroke and coxswain to steer. The whole exercise was repeated with the same teams and same location the following year in 1986 and we won the mixed team event with another banner for the mantlepiece.

Off to the starting line – in the background, the Sydney Opera House, the Harbour Bridge and a Chinese Junk

A heat of the inaugural Dragon Boat Races- Sydney *Cove* 1985

The whole exercise was repeated with the same teams and same location the following year in 1986 and we won the mixed team event with another banner for the mantlepiece.

Dragon Boat racing has now spread around the country and earlier this year, before Covid-19, I came across the Forster team practising on Lake Wallis. Despite my wealth of experience in such activities, I would now have difficulty in saving myself if the boat capsized, let alone being an effective member of the team. I have therefore resolved to watch from the foreshore and reflect on my memories.

All aboard ready for action. Lindsay centre left.

The Hunter Valley – Wine Country

In 1852 the sailing ship, "Rheinstieg" set sail from Frauenstein, Germany, bound for the colony of New South Wales. On board, were German settler families looking for a new life away from the ravages of war-torn Europe. Among those on board were Philip George Fuchs and his wife Elizabeth, bringing with them all their worldly possessions and a Sea Chest filled with vine cuttings taken from family vineyards in Alsace, beside the Rhine. Settling initially near Patterson, north of Maitland NSW, they joined that very exclusive group of pioneer wine grape growers in the Hunter Valley, around twenty-five years after Busby.

James Busby. (1802-1871), is credited with planting the Colony's first commercial vineyard on the banks of the Hunter River in the 1820s. In 1833 he was appointed by the Colonial Office as the British resident of New Zealand, where he oversaw the drafting of the Declaration of Independence 1835 and the Treaty of Waitangi 1840.

The Rhine varieties were not particularly suitable for the Hunter climate and after two years' struggle, they accepted a request from John Macarthur to join him on his experimental vineyards in Camden NSW where, together with several other viticultural families (many related) from Germany, they are recorded as amongst the first one hundred settlers in Camden.

The Fuchs Family

My wife Sandra's mother Yvonne, recently died at the age of 100 and seven months, (March 2020). She was the granddaughter of Philip and Elizabeth Fuchs. Yvonne was born in Camden and raised on the family vineyard at Elderslie, on the banks of the Nepean River. Philip Fuchs's sister Elizabeth, married Martin Thurn whose vineyard, adjacent to that of Philip and Elizabeth Fuchs, produced the first wines exported to England. The remains of the original wine press now reside in a Museum in Camden. The property is now known as Camden Estate, the only original vineyard remaining in the area along the Nepean.

In the 1850s, because of war, famine and disease, approximately half the population of Frauenstein left Germany and emigrated mainly to Australia, Canada and Argentina.(See "Frauenstein Letters"). Many were experienced "Vine Dressers" initially settling around Camden, with many moving on to South Australia as wine industry opportunities arose in that region, taking with them cuttings from Camden Park in NSW and from James Busby's vineyard.

Sandalyn Wilderness Estate

"....let the effect of being in the centre of such tranquillity revitalise your soul"

Cross Connections, Fellow Travellers and Strange Bedfellows

With a history of wine in Sandra's family, it was inevitable that we would succumb to the lure of the wine industry. 'Peppers' had recently completed their guest house at Pokolbin, and I attended the first conference to be held in the new facility. One of the sessions was on lateral thinking and on completion of the presentation and putting business aside, we were asked by Hugh Evans, the presenter, to reflect on our personal achievement for the next six months. Looking out the window across the plantings of grapes, I resolved to purchase a property in the Hunter. Two weeks later we began searching and within six months had a 25-acre property in Wilderness Road, Rothbury, under contract. That was back in 1985. The only improvements were an old war time army, barracks used as a shearing shed and 1950s fibro asbestos cottage that had been relocated from Woy Woy, which was to become our weekender until completion of our Cellar Door/residence mid-1994, by which time we had added another six acres of land from an adjoining property.

Our first small area planting of chardonnay in 1986, suffered from a lack of available water and drought conditions. There was only one small dam on the property which we rectified the following year, with the construction of a ten mega-litre dam, which did not fully fill until 1990, when we received flooding rain. This was the same year that we commenced excavations for our Cellar door with underground storage capacity.

Our location in the Lovedale area, (previously part of Rothbury), was a choice of the heart rather than of a practical commercial nature. Wilderness Road saw the first vineyard established away from the Hunter River in the late 1920s, the first being " The Wilderness," with deep and rich alluvial plains along Black Creek, where water was in constant supply. Wilderness Road has historical importance, not only for the Wilderness Winery, but also for other historic features such as The Daisy Hill Distillery, which supplied rum to the Colonial Rum Corp and the village beside the Anglican cemetery, where many notable winemakers are interred. Adjacent to the cemetery is the site of Emma's Cottage Vineyard, where once stood a church, school building and general store, all destroyed along with the Distillery in the bush fires of the 1960s. Only the church pews survived the fire and now can be found in the High Church of England building at Lochinvar. The first occupation of the historic cemetery was around 1851 and is still in use today, generally reserved for the descendants of the early settler families.

Like most country locations, newcomers to the area are treated with some suspicion and you had to earn your stripes before you were accepted as part of the community. Rothbury was no different. In the case of Mary Campbell, great granddaughter of George Campbell, recipient of one of the original 'selections' in Rothbury, we never did meet even after thirty-five years. We had made our move to the Hunter before it became popular to own a winery and in the following years many Sydney-siders looking for a country retreat moved to the area. With so many being Airline Pilots, we called the area "Flight Deck". Eventually we outnumbered the original settler families and collectively made an impact on social life and local infrastructure. Except for Lovedale Road, all other roads in the area were unsealed gravel with 'Sandalyn' and 'Frazer' wineries the only operating wineries along Wilderness Road. As businesses opened to the public, increased traffic took a toll on the local roads that had been neglected by Council over many years. Just before our first major event I checked the load capacity of a culvert near our property entrance, finding that it had partially collapsed, causing a significant risk of total failure when taking the weight of coaches laden with passengers and the consequential prospect of serious injury. I contacted Council and advised them of my concern, reminding them of their legal responsibility, having been warned by a bridge construction professional. They chose not to do anything before the event, claiming they had no budget. However, when an incident occurred, causing the culvert to suffer further damage as a result of increased traffic, Council saw the light of day and immediately found $300K to totally replace the old timber structure with a concrete pipe culvert.

By 1993, there were only six vineyard cellar doors operating in the Rothbury / Lovedale region. These were Allandale Winery (est.1978), Alanmere (1985), Wandin Valley (1973), Frazer Winery (1984), Molly Morgan (1963) and Sandalyn Estate (1985). Wandin Valley, prior to being purchased by James and Phillipa Davern in 1991, was originally known as Millstone winery, established by winemaker Peter Dobinson in 1973. This was around the same time architect John Roberts established his winery on the western slopes of the Molly Morgan Range, near the end of Talga Road. His cellar door and old timber slab hut high on the range overlooked the alluvial flood plains of the "Wilderness" and was accessible via a long dirt track up from Wine Country Drive. Tastings were by appointment only and when he felt inclined. Sandra and I took the opportunity to enjoy his hospitality in the company of friends, with tastings at the unique Millstone winery. This was a two level, square sandstone building with wine making and storage on the lower level and wine tasting bar with seating around a large square opening in the upper level floor, where you could look down on the processing below. The main feature was a large stone stationary concave grinding wheel, with a stone roller rotating around the upper surface, for crushing the grapes and sending the juice flowing into a central collection point below. This process would have been pre-industrial and unique in Australia. With a change of hands in 1999, the character of the winery was lost, and the grinding stone was replaced. Its whereabouts are unknown. The new owners, the Ross family, because of failing health, lasted only two years, before the Daven's took over. Millstone had frontages to Wilderness, Lovedale and Talga Roads. Historically, Talga Road formed part of the 246-kilometre Old North Road. Built by convicts between 1826 and 1836, it provided the first road access from Sydney to Newcastle, Hunter Valley and the unexplored regions of the north west of the state. Trade to the region was previously shipped to the port of Newcastle and the Hunter River port of Morpeth, near Maitland. Newcastle port exported the first coal to England in 1799 as ballast, only two years after discovery by Lieutenant John Shortland in 1797. Today

Newcastle is the world's largest coal port with an out-loading of around 100 million tonnes per annum.

The Molly Morgan Range was named after convict Molly Morgan who had a colourful history, having been transported to the Colony with the second fleet in 1790, then again in 1803, eventually becoming a free settler, granted land at Parramatta and Maitland. She went on to establish significant land holdings and business interests around the lower Hunter. That part of the Old North Road westward from Maitland, traversing the range was nicknamed "Molly's" line of road. Molly died in 1836.

"The Wilderness" along Wilderness Road was the site of the first grape plantings away from the Hunter River in the late 1820's. To give an appreciation of the history of the area I have included, here, an article by George C. Craig published on Sunday 26th May 1900 in the Maitland Mercury. This was passed on to me by Ron Hathaway, grand-nephew, to Mary Campbell.

"AMONGST THE VINEYARDS – Pokolbin and Rothbury."

© by George C. Craig

"There was a lot of Pokolbin and Rothbury wine drunk in Sydney on Saturday in honour of Baden Powell and Mafeking. Colonial wine has the nectar touch, and it tasted well amidst the sight of breezy flags and the patriotic sound of the guns.

In driving to the "Wilderness" vineyard, we had a chat with the local schoolteacher Mr. Mansfield. Learning seems to be appreciated in this bush land. There is a good attendance, except for a few weeks at picking time, and the children are brought on rapidly in the three R's. As a rule, parents in the bush make their children attend school well, compared with Sydney parents. Mr Mansfield is a highly intelligent teacher, and I wish him great luck in turning out well-educated boys to tackle the serious work of life.

Some of our greatest men spring from the farmers home and bush State schools. More vineyards are passed, all of them in a high state of cultivation and grape production. Although Mr. William MacDonald devotes much of his time to stock, he follows the local industry by planting a fair field of vines, the product of which he sells to his brother at "Ben Ean" cellars.

A short drive brought us up to the rails on "The Wilderness". The property is only wilderness in name, as when you drive up towards the factory and myriad crops and gaze upon the broad and well trellised acres of green vines, they are as strong and healthy as any in the district. The impressions were like that from the wild Karoo, north of which, by the by, a local vigneron of Pokolbin had been wounded.

We see that this wine district is practically represented at the front of battle, whilst the vintage of 1900 has just been gathered and fermented.

The work of picking, crushing, pressing and manufacturing was being carried out in the factory cellars with brisk activity. All were busy attending to the rich vintage. The Messrs Holmes- three brothers- know their work well, and their brand holds a popular place in the Sydney market, where the firm has an office and stores its distribution.

Cross Connections, Fellow Travellers and Strange Bedfellows

In the shop windows the product is well got up, and no difficulty is felt in getting rid of every year's vintage. The cellars are large and roomy. The cats are as golden as the vats of Luna and Cintra, the laughing girls who gather the grapes look happy and contented, and the Wetzell pan going round concentrating the juice reminds us of the old Bour and Wetzel evaporating pans of the sugar cane juice industry.

I will not pry into the style of manufacture, but a good strong wine is produced at "The Wilderness" by Messrs. Holmes Brothers. The vines grown are generally those of the district and the cultural conditions I concluded, were similar. The art of cultivation is carried out with evident system—for berry production with just the necessary shade leaf, for sometimes the vines can grow into wood and not into fruit. The branches seemed to be heavy, as the bunches were large and tempting. When the soil is clean and well pulverised, it receives much food from the sun and air.

In going through the district, I often think it a pity if those productive vine soils can get poor in crop yields, as I have seen so much of it in my bush travels. And experience. A deal of capital is invested in a well applied cellar and vineyard to make both cultivation and the manufacture pay. The old hoes and ploughs, the presses and processes, are being given up for something new in presses and machinery,

The Government provides able experts to travel, visit, advise and improve. The mark of Professor Biunno's hand may be seen in some fields, cellars and manufacture. But the Messrs Holmes are intelligent and expert themselves, and no doubt apply all improvements to suit local circumstances and conditions to arrive at the true great aim—quantity combined with quality.

The economic design of the cellar is important to save the cost of manufacture. Old styles must be done away with, for the Australian winemaker is now a competitor in the markets of the United Kingdom.

"The Wilderness" is a grand property in the Allandale district. The home is well situated, with a fine garden and orchard. The Place is like a village – larger than a hamlet. The Cellars can hold 120,000 gallons of wine maturing and matured. The property consists of 1330 acres, of which nearly 100 acres are under cultivation, the soil being loamy marl over strata of limestone.

"Daisy Hill" Vineyard *was the next plantation visited. The vines looked splendid from the road, and as we drove down the track to the house and factory, we saw the soil to be the same rich volcanic loam so suitable for the vine – rich, strong, porous, pulverised and thoroughly well tilled. The proprietors are the Campbells. The Campbells are everywhere in peace and war. They are even great in the wine industry.*

Many years ago, looking over the selectors' names in a newly formed cotton district in Queensland, I remarked there were no Campbells growing cotton. 'Oh', said the Land Agent, 'They are coming.' And sure, enough three Campbells selected a year afterwards.

The "Daisy Hill" Factory and improvements is a monument of family industry wealth and progress.

The work and business is carried on by Mr. George Campbell, a robust and reserved type of his clan, with a quite general humour about him – intelligent and knowledgeable in his profession.

His mother, a daughter of that isle "the motherland of heroes', is still alive and hearty, though she has long passed the three score and ten. Her memory can go back to the news of Wellington's victory at Waterloo. I was pleased to meet the old lady with her genial smile and ready hospitality, and calm resigned fortitude to the land beyond the house. One feels deeply impressed in the presence of old age and those who lived in the long ago, with all their facilities fresh and green. So much so, that I cheered her up with hope that we should meet again on Daisy Hill for many years yet. Blessings be upon locks of silver and the venerable.

Lunch at "Daisy Hill" was enjoyable and the stroll through the orchard with all kinds of fruit trees in magnificent growth, was most interesting. I lost my companion for some time while I found the sun had "ga'ed doun". The cultivation was clean with no weeds in the garden, and the roses were straight, pretty and even. All varieties of grapes are grown, wine grapes of course being predominant, and they yielded splendid averages per acre, the soils still retained wonderful fertility without sign of any exhaustion.

Care should be taken to maintain soil production and not let it become impoverished. I know many wheat and sugar cane fields that by continuous cropping have fallen into a state of almost everlasting decay, and the hotbeds of seed and plant disease.

The soil can always be husbanded and conserved for best vegetable production. I believe in judicious manuring – not any sort of manuring, but the soil, strength and qualities should be checked by the agricultural chemist every year, and he should be able to tell the exact manure to spread or disc harrow into the vine soils. In France, every agricultural village has its agricultural chemist, and the lightest soils of the country are fertilised by the sanitation of the towns, and by the artificial manures which can be made in the colonies for a mere song in cost. The extract manure is the best manure.

"Daisy Hill" consists of 500 acres, 200 of which were selected by Mr. George Campbell, and 300 acres by Miss Campbell, on the opposite side of the creek. The orchard is five acres in extent, and the vine area will shortly be up to the hundred, for all local vineyards are increasing rapidly in vine cultivation. The chief grapes grown are the Riesling, Hermitage, Madeira, Hambro and Pineau. The cellar looks formidable, and numerous large vats hold 120,000 gallons. Mr. Campbell makes his own wine and does not sell to the Sydney maturers and blenders.

His stock of wine on hand ranges from 50,000 to 70,000 gallons, which keeps going away into the market, where it has a good name and a large demand. The aged wine is grand, and the vat seems to have wine stronger and stronger. As you follow Mr. Campbell, he readily makes you 'take the oath' – like the Wagga manager of Caldwell.

"Daisy Hill" is the place to get your choice of wine. There is a still on the premises, but it is not worked now, as the public taste is for the rich light *wines, without being fortified. But every maker knows his trade best. There is a new stalk separator – The stalk from the grapes – and he will no doubt have a juice press, like one of those introduced at "Ben Ean".*

Mr Campbell is a quiet, progressive man who knows well what he is about. He is a hard worker -- the very type of man to improve the face of the bush and the wine industry. It is pleasing to call upon such a man and such a place as "Daisy Hill".

** End Of Article **

Craig wrote in an unusual manner. However, he gave a detailed insight into the history, people, lifestyle and viticultural practices of the time. Back then the impact of disease was less than today. Powdery and Downy mildews were inadvertently introduced into Australia with plant material from the United States some years later, requiring control by management spraying in wet and humid conditions, common in the Hunter in summer. Most of the varieties have changed, only Hermitage (Shiraz) remains as a predominant variety together with Semillon, Chardonnay and Verdelho with a mix of less common varieties such as Durif and Sangiovese.

Black Creek, a tributary of the Hunter River, cuts across Wilderness Road and the Daisy Hill Property, the high banks of which made it difficult to cross if not impossible in times of flood. In 1900 a wooden bridge across Black Creek was opened by the Mayor of Maitland, and today stands as the last De Burgh designed wooden truss bridge left in the State.

De Burgh, born in Ireland in 1863, became the principal Engineer with the NSW Public works

Department. He was responsible for the design and construction of many bridges across the Murray, Murrumbidgee, Lachlan and Darling Rivers, together with the Burrinjuck Dam and Murrumbidgee Irrigation Scheme. The area was included within the Cessnock Council boundaries after inauguration in 1906.

From my earlier experience with Cessnock Council with their lack of 'diligence' for maintaining infrastructure, and following extensive flooding of Black Creek in 1999, that engulfed the bridge, I inspected the sub-structure of the bridge, concluding that the structure was severely degraded and in imminent danger of failure. Following my written report to Council, the NSW Main Roads Department was asked to inspect the bridge. Their report back to Council confirmed my conclusions and they made recommendations for essential remedial works to be carried out within the following three months. The report was obviously filed for future action and the work was not done and a 10-tonne load limit placed on the bridge. A few months later a laden truck passed over and one of the main support girders failed causing a partial collapse. The bridge was immediately closed to traffic.

A Council officer arrived at our door to advise us of the bridge closure stating that it would not be re-opened in the foreseeable future, as Council did not have funds for restoration. This effectively split Wilderness Road into two dead end streets with the obvious effect on our business derived from passing trade. Also affected was the now popular Lovedale Long Lunch with one of the participating wineries now separated from the rest. My next response to Council was to remind them of their failure to act on the report advice and in not doing so they could not claim an "Act of God". So, because of their negligence they would be legally responsible for any losses suffered by affected businesses. At the same time I forwarded a proposal for the replacement of the bridge with two simply supported precast/prestressed concrete single lane spans, one each site of the old bridge, leaving the old structure intact as an historic site, with potentially a hanging garden to be looked after by the local community. I also provided an estimate of cost of $1.25million to complete the work. Miraculously Council with the help of the Main Roads department, found some funds and chose for the existing structure to be repaired, with NSW Main Roads undertaking the replacement of the support structure at their cost and Council replacing all other work, including new decking and handrails at a budget of $375,000. The eventual cost of the council work was in excess of $700,000, with continuing maintenance requirement for future years, plus the bill for sub- structure repairs. My proposal would have proved competitive then and into the future and provided a modern structure requiring little maintenance for decades into the future!

Lovedale Long Lunch

Prior to 1993 those wineries of the Lovedale/Rothbury Area to the east of Wine Country Road, operated in isolation without any co-ordinated marketing directing visitors to their venues. Emotions were stirred among the vineyard community when an application to build a funeral home crematorium in Camp Road 500 metres from Wandin Valley was made known. The locals, stirred into action called for the application before Cessnock Council to be refused on the grounds that release of heavy metals into the atmosphere in a wine area could contaminate the wine and jeopardise potential export markets, such as the United States. Concerns were also raised over the Queensland Government banning of medical wastes from New South Wales being incinerated in the state, creating a possibility that those wastes would be accommodated in the new Camp Road facility. The local winery owners formed a committee to orchestrate the protest, with the assistance of the Hunter Valley Vineyard Association, which finally achieved success. Our meetings held at Wandin Valley winery evolved into a marketing group producing the area's first Lovedale brochure featuring local winery and accommodation attractions. Members of the group were James and Philippa Davern (Wandin Valley), Beverly and Peter Frazer (Frazer Vineyard), Geoff Petty and Jo Fisher (Molly Morgan Vineyard), Bill and Sally Sneddon (Rep. Allandale Winery), Newton and Ginny Potter (Alanmere), Sandra and Lindsay Whaling (Sandalyn). Jo Fisher and Beverly Frazer brought to the group an idea for a group event based on a similar wine event in South Australia. Because the group were few in number, decisions could be quickly agreed to and the concept of the Lovedale Long Lunch was born. Beverly Frazer who was an artist and Sally Sneddon a graphic artist, were commissioned to create three potential trade-marks for selection to be used for marketing purposes. The now symbolic "Love Birds" created by Beverly Frazer was chosen, with Sally Sneddon incorporating the image into our brochure for the first event held in May 1994. The slogan was "Lovedale the Heart of the Hunter." With the approval of the Long Lunch Committee, the logo has also been adopted by the Lovedale Chamber of Commerce to market all tourist venues.

The first event attracted five hundred people, which at the time was a significant number for any attraction in the Hunter. Over the years the numbers multiplied to tens of thousands, becoming an NSW State Government tourist attraction of significance and winning several NSW Tourism Awards, while also becoming one of the largest true wine and food events in the southern hemisphere. Capercaillie winery, Gartelmann and Emma's Cottage joined the ranks with the latter two remaining as current participants. Prior to the members incorporating into a Trustee Company, the Long Lunch was previously marketed by the incorporated Lovedale Vignerons Association (LVA) which had its origins with the initial Lovedale Long Lunch businesses with a membership including other vineyard operators and accommodation providers.

Lovedale Long Lunch at Sandalyn Estate

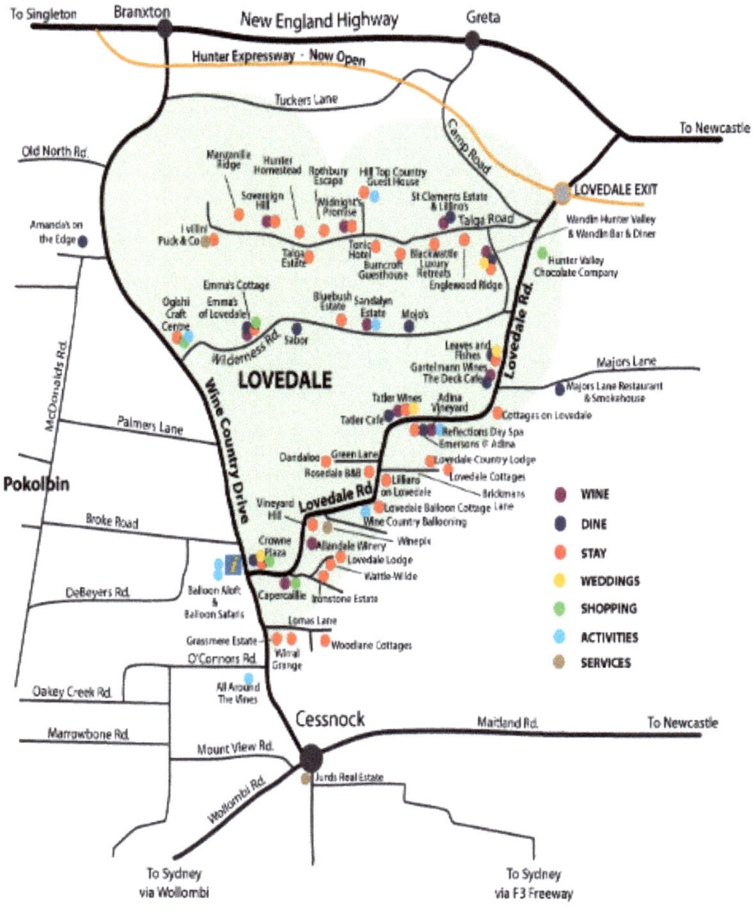

Cross Connections, Fellow Travellers and Strange Bedfellows

Lovedale Chamber Of Commerce

Membership of the Lovedale Vignerons Association (LVA) consisted of vigneron voting members only, while all other accommodation, restaurant and service providers were entitled to associate membership with no voting entitlement. Because this latter group was the majority membership, I proposed a motion that the constitution be amended to allow full and equal voting rights for all members. Most vignerons opposed the motion fearing they would lose control of the organisation and rejected the proposal. Frustration grew among the disenfranchised members who, I felt were unfairly treated and sought redress in another direction.

Through my BHP representation with the Newcastle Chamber of Commerce, I sought counsel with Chamber President, Gordon Blair, with a view to creating a Chamber at Lovedale, representative of all local business interests. Gordon also represented Business Australia and together we forged a plan to create a charter and constitution for the registration of a new organisation. At the next meeting of the LVA, I advised the membership of my intentions and called on those present to register their interest to formalise a process and seek the support of the local business community. About seventy people attended a meeting held in an aircraft hangar at Cessnock airport, confirming overwhelming support. Officially we could not call ourselves a Chamber until registration was recognised by the State Government. So, the first meeting to elect a committee was under the name "Lovedale Association" of which I was elected as

Chairman. Full recognition as a Chamber was granted in 2000. The members reconfirmed my position then as President at the Annual General meetings held in 2000 and 2001, after which I stood aside for new blood to take control and remained on the executive committee.

The principal objectives of the Chamber were to promote Lovedale as a Tourist destination, act as a lobby group for improved infrastructure, champion appropriate development and organise local events, including the Lovedale Lunch.

Members of the Lovedale Vignerons Association

Alex Stuart OAM was my successor. He and I had worked together in business and as representatives of the MBA industrial relations committee at the time of the

De-registration of the infamous Builders Labourers Federation. At the time he was president of the Master Builders Federation of NSW. As friends, we had invited Alex and Di to stay with us one weekend in the old cottage on the property during one of our regular stays, before our permanent move. They had their minds set on a retirement property in Bowral. However, the relaxed atmosphere saw them property hunting on the second day and within the following couple of weeks, they had placed a deposit on a property in "The Ballabourneen" on the Molly Morgan range, off the end of Talga Road. He later joined us in establishing the Hunter Valley Polo Association and went on to become president of Wine Country Tourism. They remain retired in the Valley to this day.

Michael Hodgetts

Another personality long known to Alex and me before life in the Valley, was **Michael Hodgetts** who had been Chairman of Rider Hunt, the international English based firm of quantity surveyors, a business, with which both Alex and I had dealings years earlier. He and partner Julia had built a Hunter retreat in Halls Road, opposite Robert Restaurant and 'The Convent', where they eventually retired. Michael, an Oxford Scholar has written a great deal about Hunter history, with an emphasis on individual stories of the convict past. His treatise on the convict building of the Great North Road 1830-36 details events experienced by pioneering **Surveyor Heneage Finch**. Michael's research into the events of the construction of the Great North Road exposes the hardship and conflict endured by Finch and his team. Finch, born in England in 1793 was a surveyor attached to the Surveyor General's Office and the son of Vice Admiral Hon. William Clement Finch. Despite his family legacy he fell out with Surveyor General Mitchell. Their relationship became hostile and defiant. However, the relics of the Finch story remain along the Great North Road for us all to see. Michael is a notable researcher and historian of past English and Australian personalities.

He published many stories about the Hunter the first being "The pursuit of Pokolbin" in 1995 and in addition to those mentioned "The Road to Redemption"1996, "Eclectic Muse" 1997, "Not King Richard"1997, "Backwards from today"2007, a history of South West Hertfordshire, and many more including short plays such as "the Trial of King Charles", performed at Oxford in 2004. He has drawn his inspiration from a wide range of studies at Oxford. He continues his work to this day.

Judy LYNNE and Peter VIZZARD

We regard pioneers as those who are among the first to challenge, endure the unknown and establish a platform with example for others to follow. There are many Hunter pioneers who have established a diverse mosaic of business enterprise, all taking a risk in their own way. Judy Lynne and Peter Vizzard rate highly as pioneers in the Hunter with the formation of 'Balloon Aloft', Australia's oldest and most experienced ballooning company, flying more than 15,000 passengers a year. At their peak in 2005 they employed sixteen commercial pilots and numerous casual staff. Peter was a former World Champion balloonist and Judy was the 1985 Australian Champion balloonist and a former television personality. She had been a presenter of 'Play-School' and later a current affairs journalist on the ABC.

Ballooning in the Hunter is a seasonal affair. They also ran an accommodation business associated with their balloon operation and in the off-season would retreat to France, where they owned a canal barge.

Biography of Peter D. Vizzard

Date of birth November 28, 1945, Sydney Australia. Titles Held:
1983 - World Hot Air Balloon Champion;
1982 & 1986 - Australian Balloon Champion;
1995 – First Place, High-Flyers Balloon Meet, Malaysia
1996 - First Place-Hamilton New Zealand Balloon Meet
1998--First Place - Nights Championship, Russia.

Peter, who trained as a science teacher and full-time balloonist since 1973, also worked on the production and flight of the first solar powered balloon in the USA and formed the Australian Ballooning Federation in 1975. He is also a professional photographer and was the first balloon pilot allowed free-flight operations in China for photographic purposes in 1985. Judy and Peter are now retired, with Peter offering occasional assistance to his old company when required.

Lovedale Radio Program

From 2004 to 2006, I produced a one and a half-hour easy listening format midday Radio program on Newcastle University Radio station 2NUR, promoting Lovedale. Business owners were asked to contribute towards 2NUR's broadcast costs with the promotion of their business. The program ran weekly from March to January, at the peak tourist season. I had the benefit of drawing on media savvy Chamber members with experience covering radio and television, such as Judy Lynne, Tony Dickenson, Bob Oxenbould and David Wilson, famous for his telemarketing and his saying," But wait, there's more! A set of steak knives!"

2NUR Station Manager John McGahan, together with Tony Dickenson were both Sydney Breakfast Radio personalities at the same time in earlier lives-John McGahan with 2SM and Tony with 2UE and 2UW, in addition to a Channel 10 show with Kerri-Anne Kennelly. In 2000, Sandalyn was runner up for the Telstra NSW and ACT small business awards, which included an interview session and award presentation with Kerry Anne. We had a wealth of talent to draw on to present some most interesting programs to our audience. 2NUR occupied around 10 percent of the Newcastle listening audience for the time slot, potentially providing 60,000 plus listeners.

In advance, each week, I would draw on this talent alternatively, and prepared the program running sheet detailing the invited Lovedale operators to be interviewed by our presenters. The number of interviews in any session ranged from one to three depending on the size of the organisation, for instance Crown Plaza Hunter Valley would take up the whole program, having a greater range of activities, including golfing events. The program was also broken up with music interludes and news. 2NUR was classed as a community station which had to draw funding from contributions and the University and as such was not allowed to advertise under its broadcasting licence.

Other commercial radio stations complained to the licensing authority that our promotions were advertising, so breached the Act and our programs came to an end, albeit the Chamber of Commerce was a community organisation. Nevertheless, the initiative, together with the Lovedale Long Lunch had put Lovedale on the map.

The Lovedale Map

The official boundaries of Lovedale as registered with the Geographic Names Board, were represented by lines drawn between four co-ordinated points and ill-defined. A large part of Pokolbin, including the airport, Lakes Folly Winery and Tourist Centre, were legally within the registered boundary of Lovedale, but locally addressing themselves as Pokolbin. One of the first activities of the new Chamber was to understand what Cessnock Council regarded as the boundaries. I requested Council officers to provide a large- scale aerial photograph marked up with their understanding of the boundary.

Most of the Long Lunch wineries were located outside their definition. Sandalyn, Wandin Valley, Molly Morgan and Frazer Vineyards were all situated in Rothbury, our mailing address, whereas the great majority of the businesses marketed themselves as Lovedale.

As president of the Chamber, I drafted a submission to the Geographic Names Board to amend the boundaries by moving the northern boundary of Lovedale to the ridge of the Molly Morgan range, westward to Wine Country Drive, following the road alignment southwards to the southern boundary. The submission also was endorsed by the Lovedale Vignerons Association on behalf of their members. The proposal reclassified the area west of Wine Country Drive to be included in Pokolbin. Name and boundary changes must be recommended by the local council to the Geographic Names Board and placed on display for objections, which came from McWilliams Wines, as a result of their trademark " Lovedale Semillon" they had registered in 1956. After some fifteen years, the Geographic Name Board confirmed the change to reflect the exact boundaries that I had submitted back in 2000. Any inspection of the internet today will show the same reshaped Lovedale map.

McWilliams Wines

With marketing underway for the 1995 Lovedale Long Lunch, all the participating wineries received correspondence from McWilliams requiring us to desist from using the word "Lovedale" in our marketing material and naming of the Long Lunch. Our initial response was to ignore their request. McWilliams intensified their interference with media and the publications accepting our advertising, promotional material and printed news items mentioning the word 'Lovedale'. Their claim was that they were entitled to the sole use of the name Lovedale in consequence of their trademark for Lovedale Semillon. This of course ignored the fact that Lovedale had been a registered place name since 1976 and had been in common usage for many decades before, having gained its name from a property settled by the Love family in colonial days.

An old iron gate at the entrance with the word "Lovedale" had long 'disappeared'.

On the 9th May 1995, we received a letter from McWilliams demanding that we respond by the 15th May with our agreement to cease using the name Lovedale. This was timed to commit us days out from the 1995 Long Lunch with some 15,000 bookings. Despite the threat of proceedings in the Supreme Court, we did not respond by the required date. All wineries had received the same demand and we resolved to take them on as a group and run our own defence, which was placed in the hands of Geoff Petty the owner of Molly Morgan vineyard, who just happened to be a QC. Together with Geoff we managed to accumulate a massive amount of evidence countering McWilliams' claims, resulting in a successful outcome for the group and all Lovedale businesses with all costs to McWilliams. Around the same time changes to the Trade Practices Act made it an offence for large corporations to interfere with the legal operations of smaller competitors. From that time, interference with our business affairs ceased. However that was not the last of our Trade- Mark disputes. Early December 2006, we received a legal letter from trade-mark lawyers representing **De Bortoli Wine Company** who had purchased Joe Lesnik's winery in Pokolbin. With the purchase they also gained the black stallion wine label 'Wilderness Wines' and some property in Wilderness Road. De Bortoli, an established winemaker from southern NSW had registered the name "Wilderness" as a Trade Mark.

Their demand was that I cease using the term "Wilderness" in our marketing and business. On this occasion I made representation on my own behalf. A copy of my response is included with the appendices (schedule D). They chose not to challenge my response and we continued the use of the name without further legal argument.

A Visitor

One Sunday in early August 1996, after the morning trade had quietened down and visitors to the valley had spread themselves around the numerous restaurants for lunch, a lone man walked through the cellar door. Nothing unusual, he settled down for our usual wine and olive tasting giving no indication that he was 'someone unusual'. After an hour or so, and with a small purchase of wine, he returned to his car, only to realise that he had inadvertently locked his keys inside, something easily done before electronic locking systems came onto the scene. Returning to the cellar he explained his predicament, so we attempted without success, the normal bent coat hanger trick into the door panel. Finding a locksmith on a Sunday afternoon was no easy task but eventually, contact was made with one in Newcastle, prepared to make the trip for a princely fee. Settling in for the wait he introduced himself as **Tim Flannery**. On questioning a little further, he advised that he was curator of the Australian National History Museum in Sydney. Some three hours later, he was able to access his car and departed.

A week later, a delivery arrived. Tim, a palaeontologist, had sent a signed copy of his recently published book "The Future Eaters," recounting his scientific findings and views on life, landforms, climate and native occupation of the Great Southern Lands, including New Zealand. His documentation spanned several thousand years past.

At the time I could not get into his work and put it aside until recently. Tim has in recent times become one of the most controversial climate alarmists and the current Chair of the Government Climate Commission. I find his current dire predictions for drought, bushfires and rainfall to be contrary to his own historical research and documented records for the last century, which show that it has all happened before, since and likely to be repeated in the future. However, his book is an interesting read when you get into it.

The Hunter Olive Industry - Don Francois

Prior to the 1990's the Hunter was not a recognised Olive growing region. There were small non-commercial plantings associated with some tourism and winery properties, providing a Mediterranean atmosphere. Establishments with product mainly used it in house. One such Grower was Don Francois who had a small grove of around twenty trees of varying varieties which he pickled and gave away to customers and friends or served with his famous dinners for his many friends and relatives. He had a keen interest in food and wine, establishing a small winery "Chateau Francois" along broke Road near Tyrells winery in 1969 and over the years, becoming an Icon of the Valley. Don stored his old wines in an assembly of large concrete road culverts creating an atmosphere of an underground cellar with bottles of aging wine laid out on racks for easy display. Many were imported French varieties and many beyond their use-by-date. He often shared these at his famous dinners where he would prepare the meal for around eight to ten guests, during which he would assemble a couple of dozen wine from his stock and conduct blind tastings with his guests. Many of the wines were past their prime but occasionally we would find a gem. On one occasion he poured a wine concealed in a paper bag and went around the table, in turn asking the variety, age, wine region and producer. One by one as the others resumed their seat and the responses had been rightfully answered, Pinot Noir, 1998, Hunter Valley etc., I was the last standing and answered the producer as Sandalyn. Don had set a trap for me with my own wine, a trap that I did not fall into.

Don Francois graduated with a BSc from St Lawrence University Canada, an MSc from the University of Ohio and a PhD from Cornell University, New York. His work on the Study of Crayfish led to a Fulbright scholarship in 1958.

In Australia he spent twenty-four years with NSW State Fisheries, many as director. He introduced disease free salmon to the Snowy Mountains, the stock of which were used to establish the Tasmanian Salmon industry. The Port Stephens experimental fisheries station office and Laboratory buildings were named in his honour. His work is honoured in the Hall of Fame-Australian Society for Fish Biology. He retired in 1986.

I now find myself selecting an old wine from my range of mainly Hunter Vintages and producers, some of which have survived up to thirty years and still drinking very well.

South Australia, Victoria and Western Australia had long established commercial groves going back to the 1800s. At Sandalyn we planted 200 olive trees and with the opening of our winery began selling olive products sourced from those states. No olive product was coming out of the Hunter, At the time the use of olive oil by the average Aussie was still a curiosity, so we ran Olive Oil appreciation classes in our underground cellars. The classes proved popular with tourists and as an add on activity for accommodation houses as a local attraction. These classes were eventually incorporated as part of our Pasta making classes which ran for more than fifteen years until we retired.

Land in the lower Hunter was too expensive for large scale olive grove plantings which became more common in the Upper Hunter around Denman and Muswellbrook where groves of 20,000 to 50,000 trees were established. One of these "Pukara", was the first to get olive oil product to market and they approached Sandalyn to carry and sell their product from our cellar door outlet. Other local suppliers came online supplying olive oils and table olives. Olive from our own tress were picked for table consumption and we reduced our reliance on interstate suppliers as with the increase in local supply and we began production of our own labelled extra Virgin Oils and Balsamic Vinegars under our "Fuchs" Label the name of which was also carried on our Sparkling wines.

Pasta Making Classes

The design of our winery was influenced by Mediterranean architecture and lifestyle and this was reflected in the operation of the business. We were pioneers of the commercial Olive Oil Industry and

Mediterranean Cooking classes in the Hunter. In 1995 we were approached by a young couple (Jane and Simon), who had returned from Italy having spent time learning the traditional art of pasta making. We accepted their proposal to run hands-on Pasta Classes from our underground cellars, which they named "The Olive and the Grape". Classes ran on weekends or by special arrangement on weekdays for corporate bookings. We estimate that over 10,000 people took part in these classes which ran from 2001 to 2018 with a maximum class size of 16. They commenced with an olive oil appreciation session, followed by an intensive hands-on cooking class, followed by lunch in the courtyard, where the participants consumed what they had made together with wine from the cellar. Larger groups were accommodated at outside venues with demonstration classes. The classes were also featured on Channel 9 "Getaway," Channel 7 "Sydney Weekender", ABC "Mercurio's Menu", Gourmet food magazines and Qantas onboard TV and seen by millions of viewers across Australia and New Zealand.

Jane and Simon, the original presenters ran the classes until December 2005 when family obligations forced them to move north to Lismore NSW.

Our classes came to an end in 2018 with the retirement of our Chef presenter Caiman Rea, shortly before our own retirement on the sale of the property in 2019. Caiman had run the classes for the previous ten years and had come with his wide experience gained in international hotels and resorts, before settling in the Hunter.

Max Brenner

On a visit to Harrods in London in 1995, we came across a chocolate manufacturer from Israel with a unique product. The London shop was their only one outside Israel. A few years later Max Brenner opened a second international outlet in Paddington, Sydney and by chance one of the franchisee reps came into the winery shortly before they opened their shop. Our previous knowledge of Max Brenner was to set us up as the only non-company seller of Max Brenner product in the country. We were part of the opening of their Paddington shop, which quickly became too small for the business and they moved to a larger location a little further down the street. Eventually, company outlets opened across the country. Sandalyn late harvest Semillon and Fuchs Sparkling Methode Champenoise were sold with their chocolate gift packs and we sold Max Brenner with our gift packs from our cellar door.

A Country Escape
Sir William & Lady Joan Slack

Sir William and Lady Joan Slack had a modest country home at Stawell, Somerset, seven kilometres north west of Bridgewater in south west England. They retreated there when not on duty in London. Hillside Cottage comprised two historic, refurbished coal-miner cottages- Hillside one and Hillside two. As the name suggests, they were constructed on a hillside and separated by a 300mm step in the floor where the two properties adjoined. There is a rear courtyard, which you enter from the laneway and under an enclosed over- bridge joining the cottages to a three-level tower, designed in sympathy with the original cottages. Guestrooms were in the Tower, which internally presented a different modern decor. When I say modern, it was Art-Deco 1920s modern. The decor and furniture, all art deco design, from the clocks down, were all designed by the great English Architect and Art Nouveau pioneer Charles Francis Voysey.

At the rear of the property they had a small vineyard consisting of a couple of hundred vines, the product of which they sent to the nearby Moorlinch winery, where we had the opportunity to savour some of the local product.

Joan, who was the grandniece of Charles Voysey, had inherited his furniture designs and later, allowed Sir Terrance Conran to copy them. Many of the Sanderson Fabric and wallpaper designs are also credited to Voysey. Joan was also a Fellow of the Royal

College of Physicians and a renowned Geneticist, having lived with African Tribes in earlier days.

Hillside Cottage addition, Tower Road, Stawell, *Somerset*

Sir William Willatt Slack KMC, Lady Joan's husband, was also Sergeant-Surgeon to Her Majesty, Queen Elizabeth. The role of Sergeant-Surgeon dated back to 1253 and Henry III. William was also head of the London Medical School and President of the College of Barbers and Surgeons (Henry VIII). Sir William died at the age of 98 on April 28, 2019.

The purpose of our stay at Hillside Cottage in 1994 was for the celebration of our son Anthony's (Tony) and Dianne Slack's engagement. Dianne is the younger daughter of Sir William and Lady Joan Slack. Tony had met Dianne in Sydney when she was representing England in Sailing at the World Championships. She also represented England on the European snow skiing circuit.

Located a couple of kilometres from Hillside Cottage is the Somerset Levels area, which consists of about 650 square kilometres of marshland and generally about six metres below mean sea level. William, with one of his sons had a dairy farm over part of this land near Stawell. When we visited the property, the dairy cows had gone, while the government paid property owners to **not** graze stock on the peat marshes. Their land had been proclaimed a conservation area, breeding ground and a stopover destination for Wild Geese migrating to and from Russia to the warmer winter climates of North Africa.

Village of Stawell-Somerset-England.
Church of St Francis overlooking the Somerset Levels.

During the last Ice Age, layers of peat were laid down preserving many Stone Age, medieval and Roman relics within. The area is rich in heritage. Walking out onto the peat flats was an eerie experience, with the weight of each footstep producing waterspouts metres away from where you were standing.

Sandra and I had the privilege of staying in the Tower as guests of William and Joan in 1994. While there, one Sunday, we attended church with them at the Stawell 13th, century Church of St Francis. In medieval times the congregation was separated with the Peasantry sitting on pews in the front and the Notables seated in more comfortable family boxes located at the back, such that they could not be viewed from below. Nothing had changed. On another occasion, we went to Evensong at Wells Cathedral where the Boys' Choir has enthralled pilgrims for more than eight hundred and fifty years. By coincidence, Sandra and I had a similar experience at Wells Cathedral, ten years earlier. However, this time, we were there to meet the Dean who would be presiding over the wedding of William and Joan's daughter Dianne and our son Anthony (Tony), in London at St. Giles Church, in the precincts of the Barbican, scheduled for January the following year.

Timothy Slack

Following our stay in Somerset, Tim Slack, had invited us to stay as guests at Cumberland Lodge in the Great Park. Tim was brother to Sir William Slack and Principal of the Lodge and Catherine's College. In 1949, King George the V1 and Queen Elizabeth R. (Queen Mother) granted the use of Cumberland Lodge to St Catherine's for the purpose of creating a modern "Think Tank" with short stays organised for delegates from around the world to exchange ideas. Elizabeth R. remained as patron until her death in 2002. She was well ahead of her time. Her residence was close by and Tim regularly attended church with her on Sundays. We had been told that on arrival at the security gates, Sandra was to wind down the passenger window and give the Royal wave. As instructed, Sandra followed the advice to the letter. The gates opened and we drove in without query.

We were staying at a time when a conference was in session, joining the delegates for meals and invited to select a good bottle of French wine from the Queen Mother's private cellar. Beneath the building, the cellar occupied a corner of a large basement, used to store many historic artefacts not on display above. Tim recounted some of that history, referring to the existence of a Tunnel running from the basement to Windsor Castle, some five kilometres distant. The entry was located nearby. However, for security reasons he would not divulge the exact entry point. The Tunnel was reportedly built by Charles the Second when retaking ownership of Cumberland Lodge after the restitution of the Stuart Monarchy in 1660.

Charles was rumoured to have kept his concubines at Cumberland Lodge and for some years after our visit, I had imagined that the Tunnel would have to be large enough to take a man on horseback, carrying a flare for light. I could imagine that Charles, having checked that it was safe to leave the Castle without being missed, he would mount his horse and gallop the five kilometres along the Tunnel, returning some-time later. After all, had he walked, there would be no point in the whole exercise. More recently there was a documentary on the ABC about Windsor Castle, and would you believe it they showed the tunnel entrance at the Windsor Castle end, and yes, it was large enough to take a man on horseback!

    Our lodgings were in the Coachman's Cottage, between the Main Building and the Converted Stables. It is a three-storey building complete with its own ghost. This was Tim's home. Out the back there is a small cul-de-sac, consisting of Houses of Grace and Favour, life tenures allocated to families in the Royal Service. Many of these exist throughout the Great Park. The three hundred horse stables had been added by The Duke of Cumberland and converted to accommodation and conference rooms by the Queen Mother.

    With the defeat of the forces of James 1 in 1650, army captain John Byfield was granted a portion of Windsor Park by Oliver Cromwell whereupon he constructed "Byfield House." Following Restitution of Charles to the throne, it became Windsor House and later the home of the Duke of Cumberland who added the stables and after whom it is now named.

Cumberland Lodge Windsor – Coachman's cottage centre

In 1995, following a trip around Europe, we returned to the UK for the wedding at St Giles Church in the precincts of the Barbican. The College of Barbers and Surgeons also located in the Barbican, was a short walk from the Church. Most of the guests were titled friends of Joan and William, many from the medical profession. Standing at the entrance to the Great Hall, was the Bellman, (Town Crier) in full medieval dress, loudly proclaiming the arrival of the guests as they entered the hall. Preceding Sandra and me, we could clearly hear the announcements, "Sir and Lady so and so," "Lord and Lady so and so." When it came to us, the announcement came, "Mr and Mrs Whaling from the Antipodes." It was all a bit tongue in cheek, as we had met the Bellman the previous evening at a pre- nuptial dinner held in the reception room adjacent to the Main Hall. There were about twenty-five guests mainly family, seated around a huge table, Sir William presiding at one end, Lady Joan at the other and the bridal couple seated beside each other mid- way on one side. The Bellman's wife was in control of the kitchen staff and the Bellman was serving wine.

At the end of the meal, port glasses were distributed to one and all, including the Bellman, while his wife had her own bottle in the kitchen. Six freshly opened bottles of Port were placed at equal intervals around the table and when the order was given, each guest filled their glass with the Port, passed the bottle anti-clockwise to the guest in the next seat and drank their own before the next bottle arrived. When the bottle was empty it was replaced by another. There were a few sore heads the next morning.

Great Hall College of Barbers and Surgeons- Barbican London

We had the opportunity to return Tim's hospitality when he stayed with us in the Hunter on two later occasions. On the first, he rang from Sydney requesting directions, at which time I advised him that his experience would be quite different from ours at Cumberland house, his quick tongue in cheek response was "What! It's not a Castle?" Before we built the winery and accommodation, the old existing cottage on the property served as our residence. The next day after his arrival, he wanted to play golf at Cyprus Lakes, so he set off at mid-day rather than early morning before the hot summer sun, when most other golfers would be relaxing over a beer or two back in the Club-House. Returning late afternoon, he looked most dishevelled and Sandra prepared a deep bath where he remained for the rest of the afternoon, with a copy of the Sydney Morning Herald as company, leaving him reflecting on the adage "Mad Dogs and Englishmen." His second visit in October 2001 followed the 11th September 2001 terrorist attack in New York. Security fears caused cancellation of the bi-annual Commonwealth Heads of Government meeting in Brisbane, over which he was to preside as the Head of CHOGM. Some official duties including the "Civil Society Celebrations" were not cancelled which meant that his presence in Brisbane was still required on a limited basis. He rang from Brisbane asking if he and his new wife could stay for a couple of days on their way to Sydney. This time the new building had been completed, offering a much higher standard of accommodation than he had previously experienced. That occasion was the last opportunity to see Tim. Unfortunately, his marriage was short lived.

Reception Room College of Barbers and Surgeons

Drago Marin Predrag Cherina
"I am living in my own future"

To his friends he is just Marin. The part he played in our life and this story could be described as one of my "strange bedfellows." A search of the internet describes him as one of the most important sculptors and artists since the great Henry Moore, to whom Marin was an understudy. Born in Osijek Croatia in 1949, he attended the University of Belgrade and later, the University of London after moving to England, where he worked as an assistant to Henry Moore. He is an Honorary Professor of the Royal Art Society and visiting lecturer at many international Universities and Societies. Marin was and remains to this day, one of the world's most prolific sculptors. He currently resides in Taiwan. Among his notable bronze sculptures are those depicting Henry Kissinger, Martin Luther King,

Federico Fellini, Alexander Solzhenitsyn, President Markos of Indonesia, Albert Einstein, Australian Prime Minster Gough Whitlam and larger than life sculptures of Salvador Dali, Henry Moore and Pablo Picasso. All these works were completed between 1967 and 1977. By the time he was 25 years old he had already had fifteen major exhibitions around the world!

7-metre high 7-ton Bronze sculpture of Henry Moore at Sandalyn

Cross Connections, Fellow Travellers and Strange Bedfellows

Some of the Works of Drago Marin Chichina

Cross Connections, Fellow Travellers and Strange Bedfellows

Cross Connections, Fellow Travellers and Strange Bedfellows

Prime Minister Gough Whitlam conferred Honorary Australian citizenship on Marin in 1977. He returned to Australia in the late 1990s with a plan for the 2000 Sydney Olympics. It was around this time that he came into our life. He brought with him from his property in Croatia some of his life-size bronze statues, together with a six metre-high six tonne bust of Henry Moore, which had been on exhibition in Washington USA. He was looking for a site to place Henry Moore with a vista overlooking a valley, similar in aspect to his Croatian property. A mutual friend directed him to "Sandalyn Estate." He captured my interest and I allowed him to select a location on the property where he was to erect his sculpture. I prepared engineering plans for the ground slab and support structure which was submitted to the local Council and ultimately approved.

The appearance of the sculpture did raise some eyebrows around the Hunter and appeared on the front page of the Saturday Sydney Morning Herald. Marin's second mention in the Herald was as part of an article on the Sculptor's legal stoush with controversial investor and horse racing identity Robbie Waterhouse, who eventually gained legal title to the artwork in 2010, by foreclosing on an unpaid debt of $60K, due to him by Marin. The sculpture now stands as centrepiece in the Banjo Patterson Memorial Park at Yeoval NSW, having been gifted by Waterhouse for which he was reportedly entitled to a tax benefit in the order of one million dollars, an excellent return for a $60K investment.

Cross Connections, Fellow Travellers and Strange Bedfellows

The sculpture resided at "Sandalyn Estate" for more than twelve years and together with the Lovedale Long Lunch annual event, proved to be a popular drawcard to our winery.

Cherina Marin exhibited a great passion for life, living in a different world from my own. He moved into the vacant cottage on the property, which he used as his base for three months while looking for, and ultimately, purchasing a home on acreage at Black Hill near Newcastle. When walking around "Sandalyn", he would return with some little treasures, picking up a stone, stick, piece of bent wire, or wildflower in which he would find some artistic value.

When not creating sculptures of notable personalities, a great deal of his work was devoted to painting and the expression of the human form in bronze, particularly the female form, which has been described by his biographers in terms of inspiring "natural rhythm, sensuality, serenity and tranquillity". We still have a few of his paintings that he gave to us as payment for our contribution to his lifestyle, including water colours and miniature sculptures, the most prized of which is an impressionist likeness of Pablo Picasso.

Marin's project for the Sydney Olympics was for the transformation of the old brick pit and dump at the Olympic site into a conservation area, incorporating a rain forest and waterfalls with a focus on the protection of the endangered Green and Yellow Bell Frog previously discovered at the location. His scheme which he called the Tower of Light, envisaged a light display above the site that could be seen from space.

Although he had the backing of Phillips and personalities like Ian Kiernan, it proved far too complex and expensive ever to see the light of day. Undeterred, he asked me to arrange a meeting with the Mayor of Newcastle and General Manager with a proposition for another project. The meeting was arranged for the following morning. A broad outline of his proposal was placed before them with the promise of full details to be provided a week later.

The following week we again met with the Mayor but this time he had called together a much larger group of Councillors and Council staff. Marin had prepared concept drawings and details for an International Sculpture Park (Peace Park) which he proposed to be located on part of the rehabilitated waste centre at Summerhill, on the outskirts of Newcastle. The proposal was for Council to dedicate approximately ten hectares of the site, where parcels of land would be allocated to the International Diplomatic Community as Embassy property and in return each country would provide a sculpture reflecting their culture. The following best reflects the proposal.

LORD MAYORAL MINUTE

ITEM NO: 16 OF 23 July 1996
SUBJECT: PROPOSED INTERNATIONAL CULTURE AND SUSTAINABILITY CENTRE FOR NEWCASTLE
FILE NO: 60/39/1/05

I have been approached by Mr Drago Cherina with a significant development proposal for the City. Mr Cherina is an Australian/ Croatian sculptor of some international repute who is responsible for the concept and development proposal of the Millenia Nexus (Tower of Light) project at the Homebush Olympic site. Mr Cherina and his group propose an International Culture and Sustainability Centre, which would capitalise on the opportunities of the Sydney 2000 Olympics to develop a unique international facility involving all countries of the world. The Cherina group are committed to the project celebrating the new millennium in a way which would leave a lasting non-sporting benefit beyond the Olympic Games for Australia and the World.

Briefly, the original concept incorporated a Sculpture Park and Museum, featuring Olympic theme sculptures from each country, while symbolically reflecting the need to maintain the sustainability of the planet in the twenty first century.

The project concept has been modified slightly, absorbing the initial feedback of Councillors from a presentation on 8 July. The proponents have also been enthused by the direction of the City's environmental programs, influencing the selection of Newcastle as the appropriate location outside of Sydney for an International Sustainability Centre. The project has been amended to incorporate:

- *An international training centre on local sustainability (providing an ongoing revenue source outside of tourism)*
- *An exhibition of best practise sustainable technologies: and*

- *A reference centre which would provide current information and displays of local sustainability in action from around the world.*

This is a timely proposal which supports the current transition in the city from a manufacturing base to a service economy.

The 'Clean Up the World' organisation through Ian Kiernan has expressed its support and interest in the project. Council staff have also received strong support from the United Nations' Environment Program for the development. This interest however, needs to be formally followed through by the Department of Foreign Affairs and Trade.

The United Nations sponsored Pathways to Sustainability Conference to be held in Newcastle in June 1997 has provided an International focus on our city, which is likely to develop over the next twelve months. This is seen as a greatly beneficial opportunity to secure necessary support for the project.

Depending on the final project format, the project could require up to ten hectares of land. Several sites within the city, including Council owned land could be considered as appropriate. Cherina's preference is for the western area of Summerhill although Kooragang and sections of the harbour foreshore and Fort Wallace offer potential.

Cherina Partnership Pty Ltd advocates the formation of a partnership between Council and the company to develop the concept further to pre-feasibility stage. This would be through a Heads of Agreement which would quickly identify the deliverables, responsibilities and risks to Council. The *agreement would be based on Council not being a funding authority other than potentially providing the site and equally sharing costs with Cherina Partnership for the pre-feasibility study. This would be implemented in two stages, the first through a $50,000 consultancy ($25,000) which would provide both parties with details on:*

- *The significance of the project to Newcastle in cultural, environmental and economic terms;*
- *Identification of possible variations to the scheme and increase viability:*
- *Concept cost estimates and project feasibility;*
- *Nomination of sponsorship opportunities;*
- *Preliminary assessment of Federal and State support.*
- *Project time frame logistics; and*
- *An assessment of available sites*

It is expected the study would take two months after which a full report would be presented to Council. At this stage, a decision would be required whether to proceed to a full pre-feasibility study which could cost up to $300,000 ($150,000 from Council or other sources.) The Heads of Agreement would be available for Council's consideration at its meeting on 6 August should Council choose to endorse this project concept.

If the project does proceed there clearly are significant potential benefits for the City and region through economic, cultural and environmental opportunities.

Timing however, is of the essence. It is important at this stage that Council consider whether it will formally endorse support for the project concept. Council is asked to indicate its support to enable the necessary development of a formal Heads of Agreement to proceed.

I recommend that Council:

1. *Give its support to the proposed International Cultural and Sustainability Centre project concept for Newcastle.*
2. *Facilitate further development of the project concept in conjunction with the State and Federal Governments and the Cherina Partnership Group.*
3. *Receive a further report on 6 August detailing Council's future participation in the project through a formal Heads of Agreement and a strategy to proceed.*

Greg Heys. Mayor

Newcastle Council saw value in placing Newcastle on the International destination map. They engaged independent consultants to review the proposal. The outcome of the consultant report was to refer the matter for a further appraisal by then Curator/Director of the Sydney Modern Art Conservatory at Circular Quay. Marin and I met with him in his Sydney office only to receive the most contemptuous response possible, claiming that it would be impossible to bring the international community together as he had tried something similar previously and failed. The report back to Council reflected his opinion and the project was shelved before it got off the ground. Today, in the climate of arts grants the outcome would probably have been somewhat different. Maybe it is time for resurrection.

On another occasion he arrived at the winery with two friends visiting Australia from the United States, however, their business address was shown as Zagreb Croatia. They introduced themselves as Thea and Berislav Crnetic. Thea, a publisher of landscape and garden books had recently completed a reference to colour gardens in the United States and had come to Australia exploring similar opportunities. Berislav introduced himself as an International Economist. They were staying with Marin at his new home at Black Hill.

Berislav Crnetic

Sandra and I found their story compelling and to hear more, we accepted their invitation for Berislav to prepare us an authentic Croatian meal one evening. The standard came up to his proclamation! Following the meal, we settled down into conversation asking Berislav to expand on his background. He responded that he was a TV and film producer advancing some of his creations which included such notable productions as "Fiddler on the Roof", Robert Mitcham's "The Winds of War" and the last film of "Orson Welles". They had tired of the falseness of life in the Californian social set and decided to move on. They had been friends of Marin back in Dubrovnik on the coast of the Adriatic

Sea, Croatia where they owned a three-storey walk up, foreshore apartment. The city had come under shelling during the siege of Dubrovnik when Serbia attacked Croatia. The bombardment demolished the buildings each side and behind them. They were in the building when a shell came down through the roof, penetrated two upper floors and landed on a ground floor bed and did not explode, leaving their home intact with minimal damage. Good fortune was clearly on their side. Like Marin, they were passionate about their artistic creations.

Marin moved to Taiwan following his run in with Waterhouse. With his new Taiwanese wife, he continued his work, attracting international sponsors and supporters, including the International Olympic committee and Soccer Federation.

My connections with the Newcastle business community and Council had been established prior to my association with Marin. I continued to be actively involved with many organisations associated with my position as a consultant to BHP and with the proposed closure of the steelworks.

Carson & Associates

From 1993 onwards, I practised as a consultant to the construction and property industries, at the same time establishing and operating the winery in the Hunter Valley. Engaged as a sub-consultant with Carson and Associates who specialised in Defence contracts, I was appointed project manager for a program that provided the Defence Department with a forward plan for the disposal of some twenty properties that would become surplus to Defence requirements over the following twenty years. The consultant group included three other specialist professional organisations being Colliers International (Property), Price Waterhouse (financial) and Clayton Utz (legal). The required outcome was the identification, current commercial value and legal implications for the manageable disposal of the properties over a period of twenty years. The recommendations were to become the basis for a Defence "White Paper" on future Defence budgets, under consideration by the Federal Treasury.

    We were all provided with security clearance to enter defence properties and a helicopter placed at our disposal for aerial observation. The properties included highly sensitive existing operational facilities, such as the submarine base, HMAS Platypus at Neutral Bay, the operation of which was planned to relocate to Fremantle, Western Australia, the Munitions Depot at Silverwater, later to become part of the Olympic site, the Navy disposals at Zetland, Military Barracks at Randwick and the St Mary's munition training facility, now covered with housing following the sterilisation of unexploded ordinance.

    All these and other sites were of immense value to Defence which was looking for a financial benefit on sale. The most notable and valuable locations were the prime Sydney Harbour Properties of North and South Head and Middle Headland. These were proposed to be handed over to the State Government, subject to increased building ratios for sites such as Randwick, which like many other properties were to be sold off for residential and industrial development. At the time, the results of our project were highly confidential, but now, more than thirty years later, all or most of the properties have changed hands into the public domain.

With Carson & Associates, I managed project planning and construction for the F16 Fighter Base headquarters at Williamtown and the redevelopment and conservation of heritage buildings and mall for the Newcastle Council Civic precinct.

The End of Steelmaking in Newcastle

The BHP Newcastle Steelworks ceased steelmaking operations on the 30th September 1999. The intention to close was announced publicly on the 29th April 1997, creating considerable controversy about the direct and flow-on effects of unemployment in the Hunter region. Within BHP management, a decision had been made years earlier and plans were in place to manage the exit from steelmaking in the region, leaving the rod and bar mills operating under a new structure using steel produced from the Wollongong Steelworks. Initiatives were put in place to attract new industry to the region, the principal focus of which was the Steel River Project for which I was engaged as a consultant to manage the project within the BHP Property Division.

Public relations played an important role in disseminating information to the local community throughout the Country and Internationally. BHP had its own PR media group for this purpose. BHP owned large parcels of land around Newcastle and surrounding suburbs. My role with Steel River was as much about marketing Newcastle to the world as it was about marketing and the development of property, requiring skills in media. My skills in media presentation and response were somewhat lacking. Together with Alan Norton, manager for BHP properties, we went to Sydney for training with the International media firm Hill and Knowlton, where we were exposed to a series of simulated media moments the likes of which you see on television every day, with TV cameras pushed in your face and questioning that you would prefer not to answer. Those media moments occurred frequently when I made an appearance in public or an engagement to speak at forums such as the Newcastle Business Club. One such notable interviewer was Jody Mackay, a journalist working with Channel Nine Newcastle and now the leader of the Labor opposition in the State Parliament.

    By the time the closure of the Steelworks was announced we were well prepared. The blow to Newcastle raised a lot of questions as to the future direction of the City and region, which required transforming its reputation from the image of a dirty and unhealthy steel city with all its implications, into a modern centre of innovation. BHP softened the blow, with a wide range of initiatives. Together with the State Government they each committed fifteen million dollars into a "Future Fund" to entice new ventures to the region and to be managed by the "Beyond 2000 Committee" of which I was a representative for BHP. The BHP workers' Golf Club land adjacent to the Newcastle University was donated to the members. Similarly, the BHP workers' Bowling Club at Mayfield was also donated to the members. The University site adjoining the Golf Club was originally BHP property and became the subject of a property swap for land that became the site of the Steel River Project. Newcastle needed a significant new player to stimulate interest. This came in the form of the CSIRO Energy Research Division based in North Ryde NSW. Before closure they had approached BHP asking for a donation of land for the relocation and expansion of the Division. At the time BHP refused the request and CSIRO moved their interest towards Queensland.

When I came onboard, I discovered the previous correspondence and saw potential in satisfying the interest of both organisations. I arranged a meeting with Dr John Wright, head of Energy Research at CSIRO. That meeting took place at his North Ryde office, where I was accompanied by Joe Andrejas, a former colleague of mine from Girvan days, who now was an adviser on the construction of the Sydney Olympic site.

I placed before Dr Wright a proposal whereby BHP would make available an area of two hectares of prime land on the Steel River site. The value of this land was estimated to be five million dollars. In turn, BHP would apply to the Future Fund for payment from the Fund reserves, thus satisfying the purpose for which the Fund was established, those of the two parties and the Steel River Project objective. With the initial expression of interest from CSIRO, I then placed the proposal before BHP management to confirm their agreement. Nearly five years after my first approach, the CSIRO moved into their new research facilities.

The Steel River Project

BHP dedicated a large parcel of land along the banks of the south arm of the Hunter River, west of the Steelworks site, for the creation of an Industrial precinct. The property was originally owned by the historic Australian Agricultural Company. The parcel comprised two precincts, the first, elevated land which had been the location of an Orphanage. The second was of mud tidal flats covered by mangroves and used by BHP as fill site for slag and coal wash waste from the steelmaking process. The area was classified as a contaminated site under the Environmental Planning Act and required decontamination and remediation before reuse. This was achieved by a cap and containment procedure making it safe for human activities.

The Australian Agricultural Company, (AA Co.) was formed by an Act of the British Parliament enacted in 1824 and was one of Australia's oldest companies still registered today. It was used for the purpose of holding and improving Merino Sheep stocks before sending for export. The company is now a major player in the beef industry.

Attracting international and domestic attention to the site, it was necessary to create something unique from the normal practice with industrial subdivisions, where land is purchased from the developer and the new owner is left on their own to obtain the necessary approvals from a host of authorities, taking many months or years to achieve.

A plan was evolved to approach the State government and bring the LEP process directly under State planning, Environmental and Ministerial approval, while maintaining the involvement of the community, Council and business interests.

The concept was intended to create an integrated twenty-eight day approval process which included never to be exceeded boundary limits for noise, air, water, traffic and other impacts covering the whole site and within the envelope, where development applications could not be blocked or stalled whilst preserving as much as possible of the natural ecological systems of the site. Significant rethinking outside the square was required of many regulatory authorities to achieve an outcome that would give Newcastle an edge in the extremely competitive international market-place, where countries such as Malaysia were guaranteeing a one-month approval to attract international business.

At the time, trade protection was the order of the day when countries applied restrictive tariffs to limit the import of certain goods and to raise budget revenue. The second part of the plan was to establish a "Free Trade Zone". This concept was also new to Australia. The system at the time was for imported goods to be held in a bond store for collection by the importer once full duty on all the goods was paid, prior to release sale into the marketplace. The Free Trade Zone proposed would create a warehouse area where companies could establish their own holding areas and no excise duty would be paid until the time goods were distributed to their supply lines thus avoiding large cash outlays prior to distribution for sale of their product.

Over time the usefulness of the free trade zone became less important with the emergence of free trade agreements and large-scale tariff reductions. Japan for instance had a duty of 200% on Australian wine, translating to a restaurant price of most popular brands equivalent to AU $60-$80 a bottle. Similarly, duties levied by Australia on imported goods have almost been eliminated.

The steelworks site was by far the largest river frontage property requiring remediation and potentially available for future redevelopment. Many options were proposed by the community and business interests, with suggestions of turning it over to the parkland for public use and bulk coal handling to a container terminal, the later prospect gaining majority support. To this end, Alan Norton property manager for Newcastle BHP and I, arranged to meet with Achim Drescher, Managing Director of Columbus Line, a division of the international Hamburg SUD Shipping group. We were looking for his support and his backing for a container terminal in Newcastle. His view was that the growth of shipping in and out of the country demanded a diversification and expansion of the current operations based in Sydney, Botany Bay and Wollongong, the former two suffering substantial traffic issues. Unknown to us at the time the State Government had entered into a secret arrangement with the container terminal operators in Wollongong, preventing the establishment of another terminal in NSW, unless they were confirmed as the operator. The agreement eventually became the subject of a High Court restrictive trade action and was overturned. However, the site some twenty years later, remains below its potential.

An International Focus

In the mid- 1990s, Newcastle had one of the highest unemployment rates in the country and by 2020, prior to covid-19, one of the lowest. The emphasis on heavy industry has largely been replaced with industry in the areas of technology research, service, medical, university, hi-tech manufacture and tourism. In 1992 the state Government in co-operation with the Newcastle City Council and private developers established a precinct of 52 hectares along the Hunter River waterfront as an urban renewal project, to become known as Honeysuckle.

Previously this area consisted of dilapidated wharfage and warehousing and now nearly thirty years on, it is a vibrant area for low rise unit developments, office blocks, restaurants with public space providing foreshore walk and cycle ways for several kilometres from Wickham to the end of the breakwater at Nobbies headland.

The marketing efforts of Honeysuckle, Steel River and Newcastle City Council, with the added resources of the Newcastle Business Chamber, Business Australia and NSW State Development, came together in a unified approach to market the region. The Newcastle Export Centre with Aus-Trade organised several Trade Missions into Asia and the Pacific to promote Newcastle and the State, in the lead up to the 2000 Sydney Olympics.

The New South Wales Government arranged the hire of Sarina Bratton's Norwegian Capricorn Line cruise ship, to be moored in Sydney Harbour as an international conference venue in the months before the Games, hosting Diplomats, leading business and Heads of State from around the world. The State Government also created a Think Tank to bring forward new ideas and concepts. In order to generate and maximise interest, a team leader of substance would be required. They found him in Edward De Bono.

Dr. Edward De Bono

For many years, one of the most influential personalities in the world was the creator of the term "Lateral thinking", Dr. Edward de Bono, who devised the thinking and reasoning tool described in his book "The Six Thinking Hats". He had advised several world leaders on "Change Management" or moving mind set from one paradigm to another.

De Bono accepted the invitation and joined the panel which met several times over the following few weeks. In earlier days I'd had the benefit of being exposed to numerous change management, result driven practitioners at various conferences and company rev-up sessions, all offering a different method of personal empowerment. However, the privilege to be part of the panel presided over by the "Master" left me with a lasting impression.

Dr. Edward Charles Publius de Bono (Born Malta 1933) is a Maltese Physician, Psychologist, Author, Inventor, Philosopher, and consultant. He is a Rhodes Scholar and represented Oxford University in Polo and Canoeing. His work is taught and practised in schools, Universities and Business around the world.

There was, however, another great thinker who made a mark on the world as we know it today. He was Professor William Edwards Deming, physician, engineer management consultant, and statistician- the creator of Total Quality management. Following the end of World War 1, Deming was sent to Japan to assist with reconstruction and played a major role with the industrialisation and the processes which led to Japan changing from a low- quality manufacturer to one of high quality. At one time or other we have all been exposed to quality control practices of ticking boxes to ensure compliance with various pre-determined standards. Deming's teachings introduced a new philosophy combining change management with quality control, without the paperwork, by changing the idea that "near enough is good enough", to creating an in- built compulsion to "Do it once, do it right". As one of the directors of the training and management support company, Corporate Direction Pty. Ltd, we embraced his philosophies and spread the word within our organisation and training offered to other companies.

Trade Missions and Richard Face

As a member of the Newcastle Export Centre, I went on to represent BHP and Newcastle as a member of two trade missions into Asia in 1998 and 2000, and Sally, my daughter, represented the Hunter Valley wine industry on another into the Pacific. These were arranged by the Newcastle Export Centre and sponsored by the State Government and Aus-Trade. The First led by The Hon. Richard Face MLA, NSW Minister for the Hunter and the second by The Hon Sandra Norrie MLA, NSW Minister for Small business and Tourism. The countries visited included Hong Kong, Singapore, Malaysia, South Korea and Taiwan.

A third Mission after the Olympics, again led by the Hon Richard Face, went to China and Japan and included a dinner hosted by the Premier of Hebei Provence in Northern China. I was scheduled to be part of the mission, but unfortunately had to withdraw at the last minute. The Premier however, who had previously shared a table as a guest at one of the Pre-Olympic lunches in Sydney, sent me a gift of a small gold plaque and a sample of 100-year-old Ginseng, which I still have today.

    Australian Embassy or High Commission Staff in each country provided briefings and contact recommendations to mission members with an interest in their particular business activity, the majority of whom were looking for export opportunity, whereas Richard Face and I had a shared interest in promoting investment in Newcastle. So together, we were accorded diplomatic access to influential national leaders, business associations and connections in all countries visited. In Malaysia we visited Port Kiang on the east coast, which had established a trade free zone like we were looking to establish in Newcastle. Richard and I were luncheon guests of the chairman of the Kuala Lumpur Race club which had wide business interests outside horse racing, including a fifty percent ownership of the nearly completed Petronus Twin Towers in Kuala Lumpur, the highest building in the world from 1998 to 2004 and to which we were accorded a personalised pre-completion inspection.

    My wife Sandra accompanied me on the second mission to Kuala Lumpur led by Minister Sandra Norrie. The Australian High Commissioner organised an official function at the KL Business Club to be followed by dinner for our group, booked at an Asian restaurant in the Petronus Towers. The function was running behind schedule, so Sandra and I left the group and proceeded to the dinner venue, to organise the restaurant for the rest of the group's arrival. Still waiting an hour later, I contacted the minister's assistant only to be advised that the minister had changed her mind with a preference for a venue where she could dance and be entertained, taking the rest of the group following her and leaving me to explain and apologise to the booked venue who had retained staff, and made a special effort to accommodate the international visitors in a private room. Naturally, I was furious at being placed in this situation without any warning and demanded an apology from the minister the following morning, on behalf of the restaurant, Sandra and myself. The apology did come via an assistant, but not from the minister herself. I always regarded Minister Richard Face as being totally professional and committed to the role of marketing the Hunter, whereas for his successor, business was secondary to having a good time.

"Faisal"

Prior to leaving Australia I had been contacted by a friend in Malaysia, Ahmad Faisal Lahini who happened to be the first secretary to Dr Mahathir bin Mohammed, Prime Minister of Malaysia.

He had become aware of our impending visit. "Faisal" to his friends, offered to send the Prime Minister's car to pick Sandra and me up from the new KL airport and deliver us to our hotel. Unfortunately, I had to decline his very generous offer, advising him that it would not be appropriate for us to upstage a state minister, let alone the other delegates who all had arrangements to travel the forty five minute journey by coach. This decision I now regret, following the previously mentioned incident.

Don Champagne

A mutual friend in Newcastle, Don Champagne and I, originally became acquainted with Faisal via his business and family interests in Australia. Don was the International Marketing Director of Ever Wood Profiles, while Faisal's family interests were in furniture making in southern Malaysia. Under international agreements, the Australian wine industry is prohibited from using the term "Champaign", but it would have been interesting to have labelled a wine called "The Don Champagne". We often joked about the possibility. As for Faisal, he also enjoyed our "Methode Champenoise" (made by the Champagne Method) despite his Malaysian Islamic background. He used to blame me for his liking of alcohol. On a separate private visit to Kuala Lumpur, Sandra and I took several cases of wine into the country for marketing purposes, without any problem. It was readily available for tourist consumption in hotels and restaurants.

The combined government business marketing efforts also took advantage of the international focus on the impending Olympics, bringing trade delegations from many countries, provinces and cities from around the world, many of which visited Newcastle and the Steel River Project. Through regular contact with various consulates and embassies in Sydney and Canberra, I was able to gain access to information services, fora and resources available for their internal consumption. Sandra and I were invited to attend functions, dinners and Christmas parties at the Woollahra home of the United States Consul General on several occasions over a period that saw three Consul Generals. Each had a term of around three years before being posted to a new location around the world.

US Consul Patrick Wall

The first was Senior Commercial Consul Patrick Wall, a State Department professional, who did not come up through the ranks as career diplomat. Instead, he had been sent to Sydney by US President Clinton. Patrick had previously been financial adviser to the White House and the Sydney posting was his reward. Among the diplomatic community, Sydney rated up there with London, Paris and Tokyo as the favoured postings usually reserved for those with a long service as a diplomat. Patrick once told me that only 14% of US citizens held a US passport compared with Australians, where in excess of 50% of adults held an Australian passport.

On one occasion I was contacted by Patrick to advise on a suitable secure location in the Hunter for President Clinton to stay on a proposed visit to Australia. I responded with the suggestion that Cyprus Lakes in the Hunter Valley could be secured for his visit and they made a confidential enquiry of management. The next day, The Newcastle Herald featured a full front-page article claiming President Clinton was to visit Newcastle. So much for confidentiality! However, the president's visit had to be cancelled as a result of the outbreak of hostilities in the Middle East.

Commander Alan Maiorano

Several requests were made of me from the US Consulate, one of which involved the visit of a United States warship to Newcastle on a "Good Will" mission. The ship was the "USS Vincennes CG-49" an Aegis class cruiser, commanded by Alan Gary Maiorano. This vessel was the command ship for the US seventh fleet in the Pacific and had a sad history as the Middle East fleet Command ship during the First Gulf War, where it had accidently shot down an Iranian passenger plane, mistaken for incoming attack aircraft. Following that episode, the Vincennes was refitted and repositioned to the Pacific, based out of Tokyo. Having organised a berth with the Port Authority, a fanfare of local dignitaries and bands gathered to greet her arrival. Most of the crew were given shore leave and I had a guided inspection and lunch with Commander Maiorano in his quarters, attended by his personal chef. The discussion centred on the operational capabilities of the Vincennes. His response to the question as to the ability to defend an attack with most of the crew ashore, was to advise me that the ship could defend itself without any crew on board. The value to Newcastle business for the three- day visit was in the order of two million dollars. The ship was opened to the public the following day. I was presented with the seventh fleet Admiral's cap as a memento of the visit.

On another occasion I was in Singapore having lunch with Richard Face and Local Austrade Representatives, when a call from the US Consulate requested another ship visit to Newcastle. Being away at the time, all I could do was to leave a message for the

CEO of the Newcastle Port Authority with the request. I returned a couple of weeks later to find that the request had been refused, he, giving preference to the big end of town, namely the coal industry. The ship was diverted to a berth in Sydney.

I was the BHP representative on The Newcastle Defence Committee, which met the following week after my return. The Port CEO was also a member and received a serve from me for letting down Newcastle business owners, who would have greatly benefited from the spending of US sailors.

The little publicised Newcastle Defence Committee was a panel organised by the Newcastle Chamber of Commerce with the objective of lobbying Government and International defence equipment manufacturers and consisted of Chamber members, Business Australia, Council , University Executive and local defence commanders and included an observer representing the US State Department. Companies being courted included Boeing Aircraft parts manufacture, Lockheed Martin (Over the Horizon long range detection Aircraft maintenance), BAE Systems (Jet trainer manufacture).

US Ambassador, Genta Hawkins-Holmes & Robert Bob & Jan Oxenbould

The US Embassy in Canberra made a request for arrangements to be made for a private familiarisation visit to Newcastle by the Ambassador, (Mrs) Genta Hawkins-Holmes. This was to include meetings with the Chamber of Commerce Business leaders, Council and University representatives, followed by a short overnight stay in the wine region. I undertook to make all arrangements for the meetings and venues, accommodation and restaurants. Following meetings in Newcastle, Genta and her husband Robert travelled with me in my car out to their accommodation in Lovedale, where I had made arrangements for their stay in a small bed and breakfast facility operated by Bob and Jan Oxenbould, who had retired to the Valley for a quieter life. Bob had been a keen fisherman and every Saturday, for around twenty years, had a two-hour radio program into New Zealand. The "two Bobs" had something in common. They both liked fishing. Robert (Bob) Hawkins-Holmes made the most of his time in Australia with visits to the Gulf country on Barramundi fishing expeditions. There had been a noticeable absence of security around the Ambassador - or so I thought.

Although this was a private visit without public engagements, security was not far away out of sight. Driving out to the Valley, a police car drove up alongside on a dual lane section of road, remaining there for a few seconds, then dropping back to a respectable distance in the rear. I can only assume that everywhere we went they were somewhere nearby.

That evening, Sandra and I entertained the Ambassador and her husband, with the Oxenbould's at "Shaky Tables", a quirky restaurant with outstanding credentials, set in bushland at North Rothbury.

A year later in 2001, US Consul General, Patrick Wall and his wife attended the same venue with us on a similar visit. We had arranged to pick them up from their Cyprus Lakes unit overlooking the golf course, later returning for drinks on the veranda following our meal. It was a dark moonless night and the stars particularly brilliant, Patrick making the comment that it would not be possible to see so many stars in the US because of the intensity of background illumination from city lights.

Other Consulate Connections

Our connections with the Consulate and commercial service continued long after my engagement with BHP. In 1999 the US Seventh fleet visited Sydney in full force, following the Coral Sea joint naval exercises. The group included two Aircraft Carriers, the USS Enterprise and the USS Constellation. Invitations were sent out for various Consulate contacts to join Admiral David T Hart Jnr. USN and group Commanders for a cocktail party on the flight deck of the Constellation prior to their departure, to which I was privileged to receive an invitation. However, other prior commitments prevented me from accepting. The Consulate, not taking no for an answer, made contact via my daughter Sally, with a request that Sandra and I join a dozen other guests on board the USS Shiloh, a guided missile Cruiser, the following month. Sally accepted on our behalf and on the following Sunday 24th January 2000 at 4 pm, we boarded 'Shiloh 'at Garden Island, commencing with a tour of the ship and then socialising with the other guests and officers on the helicopter platform. The rest of the crew were assembled around the mid-deck, dressed in full naval uniform.

The vessel was scheduled to depart Sydney for Pago Pago in the Pacific at five o'clock. On time, the mooring ropes to the wharf were cast aside and tugs eased the ship out into the main shipping channel in front of the Harbour Bridge. The afternoon was warm and clear. The ship was surrounded by pleasure craft which proceeded to escort us down the harbour towards the Heads, whereupon we turned towards the open sea, leaving the small craft behind.

All this time we had been socialising with cocktails on the helicopter deck and the smartly dressed crew had returned to their normal duties. About this time, we were contemplating a nice holiday on Pago Pago, when the ship reduced speed in a heavy swell about two kilometres out to sea, and an Australian Navy escort tender came alongside. With other guests, we made our way down a narrow gantry on the side of the ship onto a platform from where we alighted with some difficulty onto to an Australian Navy tender, eventually returning us to Garden Island.

This was just one of many involvements with the US and International diplomatic community. On another occasion, I was asked to make arrangement to book the exclusive use of a restaurant in the Hunter Valley for the purpose of hosting members and partners of the Sydney Chamber of Consul Generals, which included diplomats representing the United Kingdom, Ireland, United States, Indonesia, Japan, Israel, Canada, New Zealand and Malaysia. The restaurant I chose was "Roberts" a converted historic home in a setting not unlike an English garden. Sandra and I were guests at the event. We were seated at a table with the Israeli Consul General, his wife and two Mossad security guards who never let the Consul General out of their sight except for a short period when one of them asked for directions to a petrol station as they had nearly run out of fuel. The dinner was not publicised, therefore personal security was not evident with other diplomats.

Robert & Sally Moline

Robert and Sally Moline's restaurant "Roberts", adjacent to Peppertree Winery and "Peppers Guest House" in Halls Rd, Pokolbin, was noted as one of the most highly regarded gourmet dining experiences in the country, having achieved an enviable record of Plate and Hat awards. They originally started one of the first upmarket international restaurants in the Hunter, "The Cellar", back in the early 1980s before purchasing the old timber slab house built in 1876 and later adding an extension in keeping with the original character.

Sally and Robert have since moved to higher regions along Mount View Road, Pokolbin located at Talavera Estate, where they continue to provide a unique dining experience at "Bistro Molines" overlooking a valley, the slopes of which are trellised with grape vines.

David Slawson

International companies drawn to Newcastle by our marketing and diplomatic contacts, included Steel making interests with new technology specialised steel making packaged processes, and recycling waste into building panels, neither of which the local community were happy to accommodate. One US visitor David Slawson, whose company Stirling Energy Systems, saw an opportunity to create a hydrogen production facility on the Steel River site. His company owned the rights to the NASA power generation system that produced power, oxygen and water for manned spacecraft, using a cyclical process of producing hydrogen by passing a current through water, separating the hydrogen (H) and Oxygen (O2), then collecting the hydrogen in a cryogenic pressure chamber, and re-combusting the Hydrogen using the oxygen to produce electricity, leaving a by-product of water. This is a perfect natural cycle of energy production. The theory for this has been known for many years. Theoretically you can back your car up to a garden water tap, fill up your "petrol" tank and drive away, assuming your vehicle is fitted with a rooftop solar panel connected to battery storage.

    David Slawson's proposition came with conditions which required a Federal Government partnership and investment in the project. I set up a meeting with Martine De Wit, head of the Australian Greenhouse Office. I packed an overnight bag and went off to Canberra and after knocking on the doors of several Departments, I returned without the support I was looking for and realised that Governments were not interested at backing technologies that they could not control the distribution of and were difficult to tax.

    Later discussions with Dr. John Wright, head of the CSIRO Energy division, saw a small pilot plant established on their new facility on the Steel River Project. Only now, years later are we seeing more emphasis placed on the potential use of hydrogen and a growing acceptance of nuclear power as an alternative to coal for base load power generation.

A Few Side-Lines
General Raymond T. Roe, James Bennet

I was a member of the Newcastle Business Club which held regular monthly meetings at the Harbourside Convention Centre on the waterside at Newcastle. The depth of Business membership by private, public companies, local Government and institutional organisations, ensured a constant supply of notable and memorable quest speakers, local, countrywide and international. One such speaker was retired General Raymond T. Roe, commander of allied ground forces for operation Desert Storm, for the invasion of Iraq and now Chief executive officer for Adecco Asia Pacific. Adecco, an international business staffing company, was represented in the Club by subsidiary TAD, whose Newcastle branch was managed by James Bennet until he became increasingly blind, forcing him to retire and having to get about with the help of a guide dog provided by Vision Australia. James used to visit our vineyard with his Labrador that engaged with our cellar door dog "Bacchus", a Golden Retriever that had his own business card. Through this association we became sponsors of Vision Australia, donating wine for their annual Christmas Carols by Candlelight event at the Myer Music Bowl in Melbourne. Our Sandalyn wine bottles also carried braille and low vision labels. Sandalyn was the first winery in the country to provide this aid for the blind.

Overlooking the city, the Newcastle Club was originally a retreat for Gentlemen to relax away from the pressures of the office and home. Membership was not available to women until the late nineteen nineties, following a second vote of members, the first vote, failing to achieve majority support. With regular attendance of members falling along with the finances, a second vote was held a couple of years later and on this occasion after a successful vote, ladies were welcomed as members and the bars started buzzing again. When travelling overseas, Sandra and I took advantage of the reciprocal accommodation arrangements between similar institutions around the world. In Ireland we stayed at the St Stephens Club in Dublin opposite St Stephens Green Park. This was like taking a step back to the 1920's with an old-world atmosphere and the sound of horse drawn coaches moving along the cobbled street at night. We had a small wine export business into Ireland.

On one occasion, I was approached by a couple of business personalities representing a group within the Newcastle branch of the Labor Party, requesting that I stand for Labor Party pre-selection for the safe Federal Labor seat of Newcastle. With the sitting member retiring, there was division within the party for the likely successor. Despite their knowledge of my previous political affiliations and conservative past, they pressed me to stand as an alternative. I had no political ambition, and gracefully declined their offer.

The national launching of "Clean Up Australia" for 2000 was held at Rafferty's Resort, Murrays Beach, on Lake Macquarie, NSW. BHP was a major sponsor, and I was to represent their interest on the podium, together with John Tate, mayor of Newcastle and Ian Kiernan Chairman of Clean Up Australia. I had previous association with Ian when gaining his support for Marin Cherina's Newcastle Sustainability Park and with John Tate through interaction on the Steel River Project.

I was approached by an old colleague from White Industries. The company had long since exited from construction activities to concentrate on their coal mining interests in Australia and India. Environmental considerations regarding emissions from power stations demanded research into clean coal technologies, in which White Industries was heavily investing. White industries had some years earlier owned and operated the Ulan Coal mine and built the Sandy Hollow railway to transport the coal to Newcastle. They were now looking for a site near Newcastle where they could build a pilot pelletising plant. The initial approach was to establish a facility on the Steel-River property. However, their need was relatively short term and I committed to looking a little further afield on their behalf. I found an abandoned mine facility at Aberdare, close to Cessnock. This was complete with buildings which suited their purpose and was conveniently available for lease from the NSW Mining Union. Their process envisaged firing pelletised coal into a high temperature furnace and comparing the emissions against standard power station emissions. Their research proved a reduction of CO_2 of 26 percent, using the process and the remaining emissions capable of a separate carbon capture technology.

Over time, because of my activities in Newcastle, I found myself being invited to join more organisations, such as the Cessnock Council advisory committee, advising the Hunter Development

Committee and as a director of (BEC)Business Enterprise Centre, under the chairmanship of winemaker Brian McGuigan. Based at Kurri Kurri, the Government funded facility provided start-up businesses with low cost rental space and secretarial services until they established a viable enterprise. The centre was managed by Rod Doherty who has donated a great deal of his time to community organisations and service as a councillor on Cessnock Council.

Hunter Private Irrigation District
Brian McGuigan

The Hunter climate was not conducive to high yielding wine production, with little winter rainfall to support spring budburst and leaf growth. There was a need to drought proof the region to provide a reliable accessible water supply for the local grape growing industry. On the 7th August 1998, under the leadership of winemaker Brian McGuigan, a small group of vineyard operators formed the Lower Hunter Water Association with a proposal to construct a pipeline from the Hunter River and reticulate water throughout the lower Hunter Cessnock and Singleton local government areas. Initial funding of $500K was raised from local growers for a feasibility study, which proposed to deliver 5000 megalitres per annum via 126 kilometres of pipeline, at a cost of ten million dollars. On the 30th October 1998, a meeting of growers held at McWilliams winery, elected a committee of thirteen members to facilitate arrangements for obtaining a water licence from the State Government, the creation of a Private Irrigation District within the Provisions of the NSW Private Irrigations Districts Act 1973, and to propose a means for funding and engaging consultants for the project design. The process was overseen by the Hunter Economic Development Corporation (HEDC).

On achieving agreement from the State Government, the Hunter Private Irrigation District (PID) Board was formed in April 1999, with a registered membership of one hundred and seventy-eight growers, confirming nine of the original committee as directors. The makeup of the Committee was Brian McGuigan Chairman, John Drayton Vice-Chair, John Davis, Joe Jones, Ken Bray, Ross McDonald, Chris Cameron, Jerome Scarborough and me.

Funding was achieved via a low interest loan of nine million dollars from the Commonwealth Bank, repayable over twenty years and a successful contractor, the "Rellney Group" signed up with completion scheduled for early 2000. The project commenced with a sod turning exercise at the Hunter Gardens, officiated by Premier Bob Carr. On completion, the Rellney Group was retained as Service Contractor and water began to flow from 18th February 2000. All members had equal voting rights and allotted water allocations in accordance with their initial application, based on property size and vineyard area. In the first instance, applications were processed based on the requirements laid out in the Feasibility, restricting membership to grape growers. This later expanded to include Hunter Valley Gardens and the Vintage Golf club. The HWV-PID has similar powers as a local government council, with the levy of an annual base rate, which included supply of half the water allocation and the balance charged at $300 per megalitre. All properties were metered at the road frontage. Sandalyn had a ten mega-litre allocation which maintained water supply into our main dam, ensuring water capacity never fell below a critical pumping level.

HUNTER WINE COUNTRY PID- Pipeline Opening by Premier Bob Carr July 1999
L to R:- B McGuigan: J Scarborough: W L Whaling: C Cameron: Hon. R Carr: J Drayton: J Jones: R McDonald

Brian and Fay McGuigan remain significant and highly respected members of the Hunter and National wine community. They have dedicated a great deal of time to the public good. Together with the Newcastle University they established a foundation for Cancer research with the Mater Hospital, where Brian was a Board member and Chairman of the Newcastle Knights Board.

In 1999 I was asked by a friend and colleague Isobel Mitchell, to nominate a Hunter Region candidate for the National Export Hero's Award, to be presented in Sydney by the Australian Institute of

Export. Isobel's company, Kara Management, was engaged by the Institute, to arrange a suitable venue and to make all arrangements for the Event. Kara Management was a successful corporate marketing company, specialising in event management, with clientele including Westpac, Blackmores and Darrel Lea Chocolates. National and International Government Industry conventions was her Business, supported by a wide network of speakers and business leader contacts at her disposal. At the time, I was a member of the Newcastle Export Centre, an affiliate of the former group and I had no hesitation in placing the nomination of Fay McGuigan as a worthy recipient for the award for which Fay was ultimately successful. My last contact with Isobel (Issy) was when I made an urgent trip from Forster to see her at a Wahroonga nursing home, a couple of days before she died in 2019. Isobel was small in stature with a huge capacity for work and play.

Isobel Mitchell and Rod McGeoch

In 1990 the construction Industry was fraught with issues. We came together with Isobel's company, Kara Management and together with select associates, organised a national conference on "corruption in the construction industry". This was a forerunner to the Giles Royal Commission and was meant to stir the pot and create public awareness. Our key-note speakers were the Prime Minister Hon. John Howard and lawyer, Rod McGeoch, who went on to become Chief Executive of the successful Sydney 2000 Olympics bid company. Rod was later to become a Wine Country personality along with Nick and Kathy Greiner.

Isobel and her husband Michael were frequent visitors to Wine Country. They had a network of close friends and family. I had originally crossed paths with Isobel when I was with White Industries, at the time they took over Parkes Developments and completed the Parkes (PDC) contract for the construction of the High Court in Canberra in the late 1970s. Isobel was then, Personal Assistant to the chairman of Parkes, Sir Paul Strasser. I previously mentioned my connection with her brother in-law David Mitchell, who was NSW Manager for ARC Reinforcements and with whom I had made several trips to the Hong Kong Sevens Rugby. David and I remain connected to several of their friends, with whom we have enjoyed many a Hunter Vintage over dinner.

A Quieter Lifestyle

I am now approaching my eightieth birthday and considered to be one of those needing special protection and kept in mothballs, because of the Covid-19 virus. The great majority of older members of the community not having a disability or requiring outside intervention or nursing home confinement, fiercely value their independence and their right to make their own lifestyle decisions and I am one of that group. My wife Sandra having suffered for the past ten years with Parkinson's, which has gradually developed into dementia, is now languishing in a nursing home, with no prospect of a recovery. This is a sad conclusion to a shared and full lifestyle together, over the past fifty-six years. Fortunately for me my overall health is good, other than waiting for a knee replacement which has limited my activities, such as walking, surfing and golf.

For those like me, life goes on. I have never been one to sit around a card table, play bingo or join a bowls group. With the prospect of state borders reopening, the ability to travel more widely will be a welcome release for everyone. One gentleman in his nineties has chartered a small aircraft to fly up and down the NSW coast and then is packing his bags to drive west with a friend, to do their part in stimulating regional tourism. I too have been making the odd excursion with my "imaginary friend", into the countryside, which has never looked better, recovering from the drought following winter rain, with crops and green pastures as far as the eye can see. On a recent visit back to wine country, I found that business was nearly normal, with the area looking pristine and prosperous.

Current Connections

There are around one hundred and eighty residents living in this Evermore retirement village, some who have unknowingly crossed my path in the past. All have a story of their own to tell, some, like me, have put pen to paper to chronicle their experiences. For example, **Ron Underwood** has lived in the Forster-Tuncurry area all of his life. His forebears were pioneers to the area. He has published a detailed record of the area and people since settlement, with many of the place and street names bearing testament to the public regard and respect for his family's contribution to the area's physical and cultural development. The pioneering spirit of those families and the hardships they endured is a reminder for all of us that the privileges we now enjoy are built on a foundation of the blood, sweat and tears of our ancestors.

Nina Bathersby lived most of her life in Windsor on the Nepean River. Shortly after her marriage, her husband, a member of the Royal Australian Air Force, was posted to Garbutt RAAF base in Townsville Queensland, where at the same time, I was flight training there. Although Nina and I had never met before, we now find that we shared the same experiences, such as a devastating cyclone, the Queens Hotel and frequent weekend trips to Magnetic Island.

I also had much in common with **Leslie Organ,** another resident here, who lived her whole life from childhood until recently at Telopea in the Dundas Valley, despite having travelled widely during her married life and before moving to Forster to retire. From the age of five to fifteen I had lived at Carlingford, an adjoining suburb to Telopea in the Dundas Valley, where I used to ride my horse over the open paddocks. Again, I cannot remember Leslie as a child. However, her friends were the older brothers and sisters of my friends. Our parents socialised with the same families, the De Stoops, the Railtons and the Newports, among others. This was shortly after the end of WW2 and military equipment returning from overseas found a temporary home at Gowen Brae, Burnside, now the Kings School. The array of military equipment included Jeeps, Bren Gun carriers, Blitz heavy duty trucks and tanks. It was a playground most boys could only dream of, but for Greg Newport and me, we were living the dream and between us had an envious collection of cats-eyes marbles extracted from the vehicle reflectors. Newport's Plant Nurseries is today, a major player in the flower seedling industry. Behind Gowan Brae the upper reaches of the Parramatta River flowed through an area called "Flat Rock", a popular swimming hole and escape for the local adolescents demonstrating their "Tarzan" prowess with the overhanging branch and rope.

At the beginning of my story, I made mention of how my father influenced the development of my persona. He assisted those needing help in the community and was against those who would take advantage of them. I found myself following a similar path, exposing and confronting bullying in many of its forms, albeit companies exercising market power, individuals by virtue of their rank or position, or unions applying subtle or forceful tactics against employers, subcontractors and union members alike. Some of these experiences I have alluded to earlier.

Conclusion

We were the luckier and less materialistic generation than those following, and I feel concerned for their lack of survival instinct for any future calamity. Across our country those of the "woke" community desire to control the silent majority and suppress individual thought in favour of a dictatorial herd agenda. This agenda has become common place, aided by the curse of social media, hiding behind a cloak of anonymity, promoting intolerance, lack of empathy, hypocrisy, misinformation and vile and vicious comment, driven by a socialist ideology. I take this opportunity to freely express my views while I can. Unfortunately, many otherwise well-meaning individuals have unwittingly succumbed to a philosophy that will destroy everything they believe they stand for.

If any good is to come out of the world Covid-19 epidemic, it will be the realisation that we have to reclaim the ability to be self-sufficient for our day to day necessities and regain the ability to have an intelligent debate about the true nature and pitfalls of political and economic expansionism.

CHEERS

Some Memorabilia of People and Events

THE GOVERNMENT OF NEW SOUTH WALES

State Dinner

in honour of

Her Excellency the Prime Minister of the Republic of India Mrs Indira Gandhi

HOTEL AUSTRALIA, SYDNEY
FRIDAY, 24th MAY, 1968

THE GOVERNMENT OF NEW SOUTH WALES

State Luncheon

in honour of

The Prime Minister of Laos

His Highness

Prince Souvanna Phouma

WENTWORTH HOTEL, SYDNEY
WEDNESDAY, 1st NOVEMBER, 1967

Cross Connections, Fellow Travellers and Strange Bedfellows

Bruce & Stewart

L a w y e r s

The Manager
Sandalyn Wilderness Estate
Wilderness Road
ROTHBURY NSW 2320

Level 2
299 Elizabeth Street
Sydney NSW 2000
Australia

Tel: (02) 9367 7500
Fax: (02) 9367 7555
DX: 11543
    Sydney Downtown

9 May 1997

Email:
rrb@brucestewart.com.au

FROM

Dear Sir/Madam

Robert Bruce
Chairman

Re: Sandalyn Wilderness Estate

DIRECT LINE

Our client has brought our attention to certain articles published in the Autumn 1997 edition of "Wine Hunter" (pages 24-29) and in a recent publication of "Vogue Entertaining" relating to the use of the word "Lovedale". Secondly, it has provided us with a brochure in the nature of an invitation to attend a function "Lovedale Hunter Valley Long Lunch" on 17 & 18 May 1997. The latter being "a promotion of the Hunter Valley Wine Country Visitors Centre in conjunction with the Lovedale Wineries and Vineyards".

9367 7524

OUR REF

RRB:3597

We are writing to you on the basis that as the proprietor of the above business, you have been associated with the publication of such articles and assert to be classified as one of the "Lovedale Wineries and Vineyards".

RRB0905e.tsc

Our client has traded since 1877 and has had a long association with the term "Lovedale".

- As a Trademark. In September 1956 our client sought registration in Class 33, Australia of the word "Lovedale" which was officially granted on 9 January 1958. Registration is still current A129,432 and our client also holds registration for the mark in New Zealand. When our client made application for the Trademark in 1956 a search was

Affiliated Firms
Melbourne
Rogers & Gaylard
Adelaide
Gun & Davey

Cross Connections, Fellow Travellers and Strange Bedfellows

**Commercial Service
U.S. Department of Commerce**

Sydney Australia

February 11, 1999

Mr. Lindsay Whaling
Project Manager
Steel River Project
BHP Steel
PO Box 196B
Newcastle NSW 2300

Dear Lindsay:

Thank you very much for the luncheon on Monday, good company and lively conversation.

It was a pleasure seeing Isobel again and I look forward to working with you both on future projects and events.

Kind regards,

Patrick T. Wall
Principal Commercial Officer

In USA reply to:
American Consulate General (Sydney)
PSC 280
Unit 11024
APO AP 96554-0002

Tel (02) 9373 9200
Fax (02) 9221 0573

The Commercial Service
Level 59, MLC Centre
19-29 Martin Place
Sydney NSW 2000

Cross Connections, Fellow Travellers and Strange Bedfellows

**Commercial Service
U.S. Department of Commerce**

Sydney Australia

February 11, 1999

Mr. Lindsay Whaling
Project Manager
Steel River Project
BHP Steel
PO Box 196B
Newcastle NSW 2300

Dear Lindsay:

Thank you very much for the luncheon on Monday, good company and lively conversation.

It was a pleasure seeing Isobel again and I look forward to working with you both on future projects and events.

Kind regards,

Patrick T. Wall
Principal Commercial Officer

In USA reply to:
American Consulate General (Sydney)
PSC 280
Unit 11024
APO AP 96554-0002

Tel (02) 9373 9200
Fax (02) 9221 0573

The Commercial Service
Level 59, MLC Centre
19-29 Martin Place
Sydney NSW 2000

Cross Connections, Fellow Travellers and Strange Bedfellows

CONSULATE
OF THE
UNITED STATES OF AMERICA

Mr Lindsay Whaling
Project Manager
BHP Steel
P O Box 196B
Newcastle NSW 2300

10 JUL 1999

Dear Mr Whaling

I am writing to draw your attention to an important event being organised by the Premier and Government of New South Wales of which I am an active supporter.

On 5th and 6th August this year, the New South Wales Government will host the first ever Australian/United States Business Leaders' Forum. This unprecedented event will bring together business leaders from both countries to create new opportunities for business.

The Forum, which will be held at Darling Harbour Exhibition and Convention Centre, has attracted participants and speakers of the highest international calibre including:

- Paul Volcker – former Chairman of the US Federal Reserve Bank;
- William Clark – former US Assistant Secretary of State and President of the Japan Society;
- Phil Scanlan – CEO of Bonlac Foods and Convenor of the American/Australian Leadership Dialogue;
- Paul Anderson – CEO of BHP Australia;
- William Ferguson – MD of Citibank NA Australia;
- The Hon Susan Golding – Mayor of San Diego;
- Peter Farrell – MD, ResMed, San Diego.

It has been scheduled to coincide with the Weekend Festival of Football, featuring games of Rugby League on Friday August 6, Australian Rules on Saturday August 7 and, the finale:

The first ever American Bowl football game in the Southern Hemisphere: the Denver Broncos (current Super Bowl champions) vs the San Diego Chargers at Stadium Australia on Sunday 8 August.

I urge you not to miss the Forum. It has the potential to generate tremendous business opportunities for enterprising firms well into the next century.

Enclosed is an information booklet and application form. I hope I will see you there in August. If you are unable to attend, please pass the attached to a colleague who may be interested.

Sincerely,

Richard L. Greene
U.S. Consul General

Cross Connections, Fellow Travellers and Strange Bedfellows

20/2/01

CONSUL GENERAL OF THE
UNITED STATES OF AMERICA
SYDNEY, AUSTRALIA

Sandra & Lindsay

Patricia and I had a wonderful time in the Hunter. Thank you so much for the hospitality you extended to us. I am just sorry that I did not visit earlier!

Regards and see you in Sydney

Michel J'eze

(In case you did not have a moments from your Lake Erie trip, I thought that you would appreciate the card)

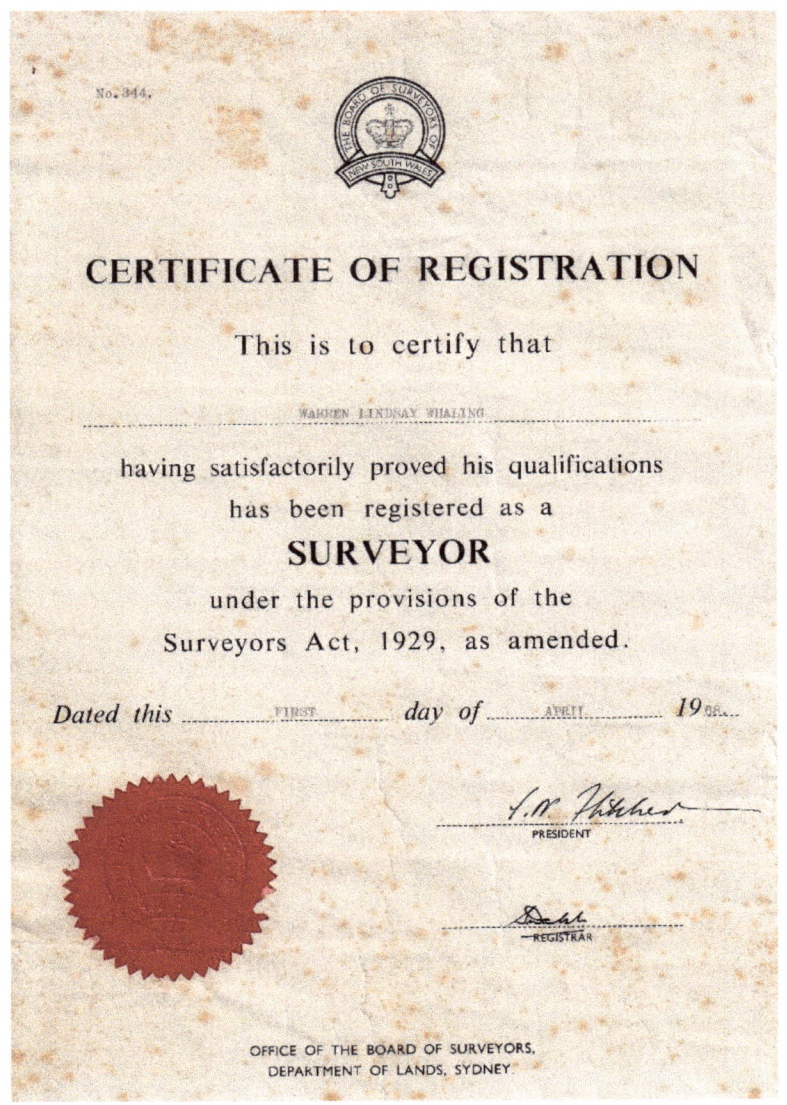

TOMMY G. THOMPSON

Governor
State of Wisconsin

November 29, 1999

Ms. Lindsay Whaling
Sandalyn Wilderness Estate
Wilderness Road
Rothbury NSW 2321
AUSTRALIA

Dear Ms. Whaling:

I would like to express my sincere appreciation for the gracious hospitality extended to me on my recent trade mission to Australia. The people of Australia are understandably proud of their rich heritage and beautiful country, thank you for sharing it with me and the members of the Wisconsin trade delegation.

I look forward to future trips to Australia and also to hosting you in Wisconsin if your travels ever allow. Again, thank you for your gracious hospitality.

Sincerely,

TOMMY G. THOMPSON
Governor, State of Wisconsin

TGT/nmb

Cross Connections, Fellow Travellers and Strange Bedfellows

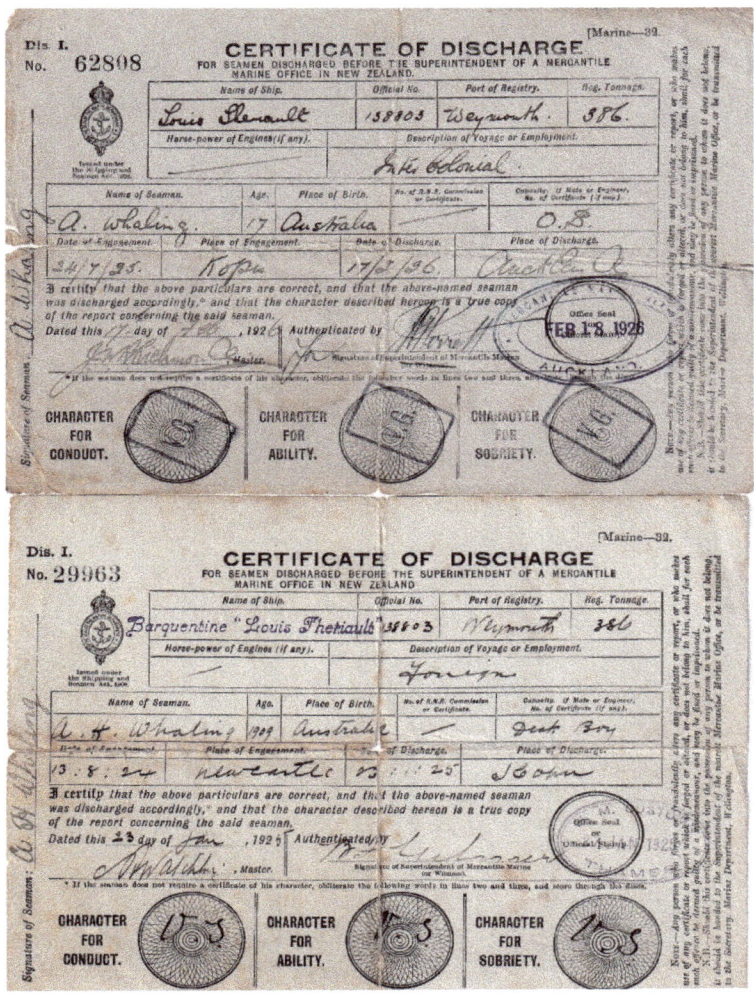

 **Commercial Service
U.S. Department of Commerce**

Sydney Australia

April 10, 2000

Mr. Lindsay Whaling
Project Manager, Steel River Project
Rod, Bar & Wire Division
BHP Steel
PO Box 196B
Newcastle, NSW 2300

Dear Lindsay:

Thank you very much for all the time and hospitality you spent on us during our recent visit to Newcastle. Plainly, the meetings we had and the contacts we made could not have happened without you. I hope that someday soon I can get up to the Hunter Valley for a few days to get to know the region better (and, of course, imbibe some more wine).

All the best to you and your family. I look forward to seeing you again soon.

Regards,

James M. McCarthy
Deputy Senior Commercial Officer

In USA reply to:
American Consulate General (Sydney)
PSC 280
Unit 11024
APO AP 96554-0002

Tel: (02) 9373 9200
Fax: (02) 9221 0573

www.csaustralia.org

The Commercial Service
Level 59, MLC Centre
19-29 Martin Place
Sydney NSW 2000

Cross Connections, Fellow Travellers and Strange Bedfellows

EMBASSY OF THE
UNITED STATES OF AMERICA

Canberra, Australia
April 14, 2000

Mr. Lindsay Whaling
Project Manger, Steel River Project
Rod, Bar & Wire Division
BHP Steel
P.O. Box 196B
Newcastle, NSW 2300

Dear Mr. Whaling:

I wanted to take a moment and thank you for your excellent support during our recent trip to Newcastle. The meetings were insightful and your time and hospitality were greatly appreciated. Please give our warmest wishes to your wife as well.

Sincerely,

Genta Hawkins Holmes
Ambassador

United States Information Service
CONSULATE GENERAL OF THE UNITED STATES OF AMERICA
Level 59 - MLC Centre, 19-29 Martin Place, Sydney, NSW 2000
Tel: 02-373-9200. Fax: 02-221-0551

You are cordially invited to attend a luncheon and tour of the

USS Benfold

on
Thursday, January 29, 1998
12:30 p.m.

at
Fleet Base #2
Cowper Road, Woolloomooloo

The USS Benfold, a modern destroyer of the "AEGIS" class, is paying a port visit to Sydney from January 28 thru January 31. Commanding Officer Donald Michael Abrashoff will be hosting a luncheon for invited guests. The 12:30 p.m. to 1:30 p.m. luncheon will be followed by a 45-minute tour of the ship.

Parking will be available on Fleet Base. Your prompt arrival will be appreciated. I hope you will be able to join us and look forward to seeing you.

Kathleen Reilly
Deputy Director

RSVP by January 23 to Kathy Topley, tel: 9373 9222; fax: 9221 0551

Cross Connections, Fellow Travellers and Strange Bedfellows

**Commercial Service
U.S. Department of Commerce**

Sydney Australia

On behalf of
Cdr. Chuck J. Pierce, USN
Commanding Officer of USS Crommelin

The U.S. Consulate General, Sydney
cordially invites

Lindsay Whaling

to attend a luncheon
on board the USS Crommelin

on Wednesday, August 5, 1998.

A tour of the ship
shall commence at 11:30 a.m.
Followed by luncheon
at 12:30 p.m.

Berth No.5, Lee Wharf
Newcastle

RSVP: Jan Starling/Phil Keeling
Wednesday, July 29, 1998
(02) 9373-9205

In USA reply to: American Consulate General (Sydney) PSC 280 Unit 11024 APO AP 96554-0002	Tel (02) 9373 9200 Fax (02) 9221 0573	The Commercial Service Level 59, MLC Centre 19-29 Martin Place Sydney NSW 2000

Cross Connections, Fellow Travellers and Strange Bedfellows

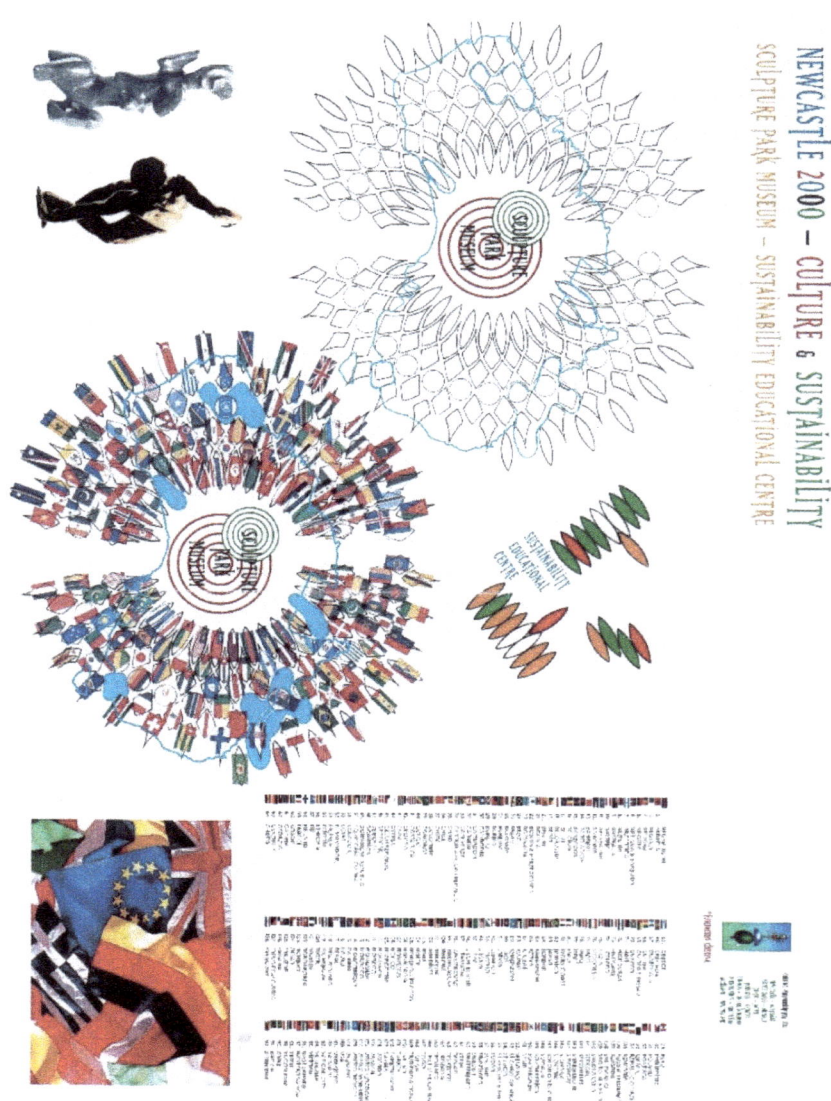

Cross Connections, Fellow Travellers and Strange Bedfellows

Cross Connections, Fellow Travellers and Strange Bedfellows

1.MAR.2001 16:33   US&FCS THE COMMERCIAL SERVICE   NO.632   P.1

CONSULATE GENERAL OF THE
UNITED STATES OF AMERICA

Level 59, MLC Centre
19-29 Martin Place
SYDNEY NSW 2000
Phone: 9373-9200
Admin Fax: 9373-9125
Visa Fax: 9373-9184

In U.S.A. reply to:
American Consulate General (Syd)
PSC 280, Unit 11026
APO AP 96554-0002

To: Mr & Mrs Lindsay Whaling
     Sandalyn Wilderness Estate
Fax: 02-4930 7611

Date: February 27, 2001

Subject: **INVITATION TO RECEPTION**
Number of pages including this cover sheet: 1

Dear Mr & Mrs Whaling,

The Consul General of the United States of America and Mrs Greene

request the pleasure of your company

at a Reception to meet the members of the

West Virginia Trade Mission to Australia

on Monday, March 5, 2001

at 6.00pm-8.00pm

R.S.V.P.   Place: Statford
02-9373 9205   20 Wallaroy Road
                                Double Bay

Cross Connections, Fellow Travellers and Strange Bedfellows

NEW SOUTH WALES

MINISTER FOR GAMING AND RACING
Minister Assisting the Premier on Hunter Development

Please reply to Newcastle Office
Level 4, 251 Wharf Road, Newcastle NSW 2300
Ph: 49278799   Fax: 49278798
Ref: GB

INTRODUCING: Mr Lindsay Whaling
Proprietor
Sandalyn Wilderness Estate

Due to commitments with the Sydney Olympic Games I am unable on this occasion to lead the Hunter Business Mission to Asia. I am therefore providing this introductory letter for Mr Lindsay Whalings, Proprietorm Sandalyn Wilderness Estate, Wilderness Road, Rothbury, NSW, 2321 during his overseas visit to Hong Kong, Malaysia and Singapore as a member of the Hunter Business Mission.

Sandalyn Estate in the Lovedale area of the Hunter Valley, is fast gaining a reputation as one of the Valley's finest premium wine producers of red, white and sparkling wines. With 20 acres under vine, each year they continue to receive critical acclaim for their wine.

In his current visit overseas I would deeply appreciate anything which can be done to assist Mr Whalings in the fulfilment of his commitments, visits to places and events of special interest and in the carrying out of his itinerary.

This letter of introduction is given to Mr Whalings, by me, in my capacity as the elected Member of the New South Wales Parliament for the electorate of Charlestown and as the Minister for Gaming and Racing and Minister Assisting the Premier on Hunter Development in the Legislative Assembly of New South Wales.

GIVEN UNDER MY SIGNATURE
AT NEWCASTLE
19 July 2000   19/7/00

The Hon. J Richard Face, MP
Member for Charlestown
Minister for Gaming and Racing and
<u>Minister Assisting the Premier on Hunter Development</u>

Level 13, 55 Hunter Street, Sydney 2000, NSW, Australia
Telephone (02) 9237 2555, Facsimile (02) 9237 2500
Email mindgr@ozemail.com.au

Cross Connections, Fellow Travellers and Strange Bedfellows

COMMANDING OFFICER
USS VINCENNES (CG-49)

March 26, 1998

Mr. and Mrs. Lindsay Whaling
Wilderness Road Rothbury
Hunter Valley 2321
NSW Australia

Dear Lindsay and Sandra,

I want to thank you both for your generous hospitality during VINCENNES' port visit to Newcastle. From the moment we arrived, Newcastle made us feel welcome and at ease. I was glad you were able to attend the reception on Friday night. It was a wonderful evening and I hope you enjoyed it as much as we did.

My day spent with you in Hunter Valley was truly a special and memorable experience. *Sandalyn* is a paradise that most would only dream about. I commend your drive to pursue your dream. To be honest, I had never fully comprehended the amount of hard work required to produce a great wine. Your success is obvious by the wine we sampled.

Newcastle will always be special to us. I have rarely seen a ship and its crew treated so well and enjoy themselves so much. You are certainly fortunate to live near such a beautiful and magnificent place. I may still find a way to defect there (and I'll look to you to find me a job, Lindsay!)

Upon departing Newcastle, we had a safe and scenic voyage to Townsville. A fitting conclusion to a tremendous visit. Thank you again for your hospitality. We enjoyed giving Sally and John a tour of our ship. Enjoy your "Admiral's cap". We wish you all Fair Winds and Following Seas.

Warm regards,

Al

Alan G. Maiorano
Commander, U.S. Navy

Appendix 1
Eulogy for KEVIN RAYMOND SHEATHER

Husband and life partner to Pam, Father to Michelle and Nicole, Grandfather, respected businessman. A True Friend to many here today.

Some friendships come and go, while others last and evolve over a lifetime. In the case of Sandra and me, Pam and Kevin came into our lives, initially from a mid-life business connection, enduring both time and distance.

My first contact with Kevin was around thirty-five years ago when I commenced employment with Girvan Bros in the early 1980s. Kevin R Sheather Electrical Pty Ltd was already established as a reliable electrical contractor with several Girvan projects prior to my arrival.

The 1980s was a time when deals were done over a long lunch and confirmed with a hand-shake. It was the time of Alan Bond and the rise and fall of corporations and the stock exchange. I can remember one such long lunch when Kevin and I shook hands over a contract confirming the price on the back of a postage stamp, prior to a more formal documentation. As time went by the business association evolved into a more personal relationship including family, with invitations to Sheather Christmas parties at Mortlake and at Pam and Kevin's homes in Castle Circuit North Balgowlah and Burran Ave Mosman. Kevin was held in high regard by his business associates, competitors, employees and friends alike.

Sandra and I regarded Number 5 Burran Avenue Mosman as the Mosman Hilton, where we enjoyed the hospitality of Pam and Kevin. On many occasions we entered via the garage, which one could have easily mistaken for a Mercedes Benz dealership, walked to the lift at the rear, stopping only at mid-level for a quick sortie into the wine cellar to select a bottle of red to enjoy with dinner. Afterwards, we would retire to our room overlooking the pool and gardens, equal in comfort to the most prestigious international hotels.

In June 2007, I found myself in St Vincent's Hospital for knee replacement surgery. Sandra was left in the Hunter to look after the Cellar Door with Sally to pick me up on discharge. What we did not plan for was the deep low depression weather system that formed off the coast, causing extensive flooding in Sydney and the Hunter, cutting access between. Sally could not drive down to pick me up, leaving me stranded at St Vincent's. Again Pam and Kevin came to the rescue, picking me up and providing me with a couple of days respite at the Mosman Hilton until the weather normalised, allowing me to return home.

I have recently completed a book, which in part includes a section on Kevin. I had intended that the title was to be "Crossed Connections and Strange Bedfellows." However. my "Editor" Lorraine "nagged" me into changing the title, as she thought that readers might get the wrong impression and I have since changed it to "Cross Connections and Fellow Travellers," under which heading, my friendship with Kevin fits more comfortably.

Kevin's part in the book relates largely to a project in Queensland, the Toowong Shopping Centre, for which Kevin Sheather Queensland had contracted the electrical installation. By any measure this was a large contract and when the construction fell well behind the targeted completion date, I was sent back to Queensland to resolve the many industrial issues with Unions and unresolved sub- contractor variation claims. Successfully negotiating the unions to return to work, I then started on the sub-contractors. The project was three months behind program and six months to go, with a weekly default penalty of $500K with David Jones, the main tenant. Sheather Electrical Queensland did not have the resources to fast-track completion, so I rang Kevin in Sydney and gave him the ultimatum-"I want 20 additional electricians on site, and I want them tomorrow!" The following day, he flew 20 electricians from Sydney. The project was completed on the day we had committed to three years prior, an achievement that could not have been realised without the support of Kevin and his crew. That was a true test of friendship, which has remained solid to this day.

    In 1994, Sandra and I relocated to the Hunter Valley property we had purchased back in 1985 and where we were establishing a small winery business. I remained active in the construction industry in Newcastle as a consultant to BHP, Defence Industry, and others. With construction of our Cellar Door Facility, Kevin came to the rescue once again giving us "mates' rates" for the electrical installation of the winery. By coincidence, the Italian wall lights happened to be the same as those of the refurbished Intercontinental Hotel at Circular Quay in Sydney (one of Sheather-Girvan contracts). Let us, just call it an 'over order'.

Pam and Kevin also joined us in the Hunter, taking home with them a few "samples" of the local product. I am curious, however, as to the contents of the Burran Ave, wine cellar. **Did they really drink it all before they sold?**

KEVIN-you have been a good and faithful friend. In future, when a storm passes over, I will imagine you keeping your hand in at the lightning control panel. Farewell!

Appendix 2
Profile of
Warren Lindsay Whaling

With Sandra my wife we established Sandalyn Wilderness Estate in 1985, the name being derived from 'Sandra & Lindsay'. Sandra's credentials with winemaking in Australia date back to 1852 when her Great Grandfather Phillip Fuchs and family settled near Maitland, bringing with them vines from vineyards in Alsaise. After two years, Governor John McArthur requested they move to experimental vineyards at Camden Park Estate. Sandra's pre cellar door experience includes manager and buyer for fashion and fabric retail outlets in Sydney.

Sandalyn now in its 20th year has uniquely positioned itself as a tourist destination, actively promoting the virtues of the boutique industry supporting our lifestyle. Sandalyn has been a leader with the emerging Olive Industry and a Provedore of fine Australian Olive Oils for twelve years, more recently the awards for the inaugural Hunter Valley Olive Oil Show, presented at Sandalyn.

As a point of difference, Sandalyn conducts Olive Oil tastings and conducts Olive Oil appreciation and Pasta making classes every weekend. Visitors arriving especially for these activities generate opportunity for other businesses in the region. These activities have been widely shown on TV and various forms of the Media. In 2000 Sandalyn was runner-up in the NSW/ACT Australia Post Small Business Awards.

Date: September 2005

www.ingramcontent.com/pod-product-compliance
Lightning Source LLC
Chambersburg PA
CBHW051537010526
44107CB00064B/2760